PREPSKILLS ® INC.

American College Admissions Guide for Canadians

www.PREPSKILLS.com

SIXTH EDITION

ISBN# 978-1988118017

TABLE OF CONTENTS

INTRODUCTION

WHERE DO I BEGIN?

One the most difficult things about applying to college in the United States is figuring out where to begin.

Oftentimes, your school counsellor will be more familiar with guiding you through the application procedures for Canadian universities and colleges. It's important to keep in mind that applications for American universities often bring into play a whole slew of considerations and obligations not necessary for Canadian institutions.

- Did you know that American universities look at all your grades, from Grade 9 onwards. While most Canadian universities only look at your Grade 11 and Grade 12?

- Did you know that most; but not all, American universities require that you write the SAT or ACT, while most Canadian universities do not?

- Did you know that full-tuition sports scholarships are only available at American colleges and not at Canadian colleges?

There are many differences between Canadian and American universities. Those differences have little to do with the quality of education that you will receive in either country. Rather, they relate to the differing funding and organizational structures of the institutions in question. This manual is meant to help you understand and appreciate those differences so that you can, more effectively, apply for entry as an undergraduate to your college of choice.

Canada versus the United States

To start, it helps to note, the biggest difference between Canadian and American post-secondary institutions. In Canada, all universities, except for a rare few, are publicly subsidized. That means that although it costs the university about $18,000 to $23,000 to educate you for one year, *you* only have to pay about $4,000 to $7,000, a year, in tuition costs, the rest is covered by the government, i.e. taxpayers. In other countries, such as Ireland and Scotland, the government pays for all the tuition costs, students pay no tuition.

In the United States, the reverse is generally the case. Although state-level universities do get public subsidizations, many colleges and universities in the U.S.A. are entirely "private." That means you, the student, must pay for your entire tuition. Depending on the size of the institution, the diversity of courses offered, the location of the school, and the profit margin that each university is looking to generate, your tuition can range anywhere from $10,000 to $40,000 a year.

In trying to figure out which university or college you want to attend, it helps to remember that tuition fees do not necessarily relate to the quality of teaching. So before deciding which colleges you want to apply to, make sure to consider a variety of factors.

Ask yourself the following questions:

- Does this school offer the program I want?
- Will I have to settle for a program that isn't exactly what I hoped for?
- Does this school offer a high teacher-to-student ratio or will I just be another number in the crowd?
- Is this school located in a city or town I want to live in, or will I find myself socially isolated?

These are just a few considerations you should keep in mind while navigating through the complex world of college admissions. In a later section, we will discuss detailed considerations you take into account when choosing a college.

Take a few minutes to flip through this manual and identify the sections that apply to you. Being prepared with an understanding of how American colleges work and how they judge differing applicants is half the battle.

So let's get started.

HOW TO USE THIS MANUAL?

This manual is meant to help you become familiar with the admissions procedures for American colleges. It clarifies some of the basic concepts related to the American university and college systems, and it points you in the right direction when it comes to important issues, such as entrance exams, money for school, and sports funding.

Each section in this manual is self-contained, meaning you can appeal to it for specific information without having to read through the rest of the guide.

If you want to be fully prepared for your application journey, we recommend you read through the entire PREPSKILLS® *US Admissions Guide for Canadians* and try some of the websites recommended in each section.

DEFINING "COLLEGE"

So, you're considering going to the United States for your post-secondary studies. At first, the application and admissions process can seem unwieldy and confusing. The first thing you should do is prepare yourself with some basic conceptual definitions that will help you demystify the American college system.

WHAT IS THE DIFFERENCE BETWEEN A "COLLEGE" AND A "UNIVERSITY"?

In Canada, Britain, Australia, and other English-speaking countries around the world, the term "university" equates to institutions that offer 4-year post-secondary degrees, while the term "college" typically refers to trade, vocational, and technical schools.

However, in the American context, both "college" and "university" refer to 4-year, degree granting, post-secondary institutions. They also refer to 2-year, degree granting, community institutions. From an educational point of view, there is almost no difference between a "college" and a "university". In the U.S., both terms are used to refer to post-secondary degree-granting institutions.

In general, "colleges" in the U.S. tend to be entirely private institutions with smaller student bodies, while "universities" are often publicly-funded (e.g. state universities), and tend to have much larger and more diverse student bodies.

HOW MANY COLLEGES AND UNIVERSITIES ARE THERE IN THE UNITED STATES?

There are more than 4,400 accredited colleges and universities in the United States. They vary in size, scope, and location. It's worthwhile noting the following categorizations, as they constitute distinct groups within the American post-secondary educational community: Ivy League colleges, public colleges, liberal arts colleges, and community colleges.

Ivy League colleges

"Ivy League" is often thrown around without much definition these days. Did you know that "Ivy League" is actually a sports reference, not an academic one?

The term "Ivy League" was first used by American sports writers in the 19th century to distinguish sports teams from older colleges and collegiates. Those writers invoked the metaphor of "ivy" a symbol of old age, since the colleges in question were amongst the country's oldest.

The "Ivy League" of colleges—all of which are located in the north-eastern corner of the United States—were formed as a sports community (also known as an "athletic conference"). The term was officially recognized in sports vocabulary in 1954, when college football was popularized.

"Ivy League" now evokes connotations of social elitism. Apart from Cornell, all of the Ivy League colleges were created in the colonial era. They were established prior to the American Revolution. At the time, they catered solely to white, English, upper-class students. They have long served wealthy families and their children—hence the traditional association of "Ivy League" with social elitism. Not surprisingly, these schools are all private, except for Cornell, which does receive some state funding.

Since the 19th century, however, Ivy League schools have changed in important ways. They now boast some of the world's largest private endowment funds—i.e. funds comprised of donations made by individuals. Harvard's endowment fund is the world's largest, at about $37.6 billion USD as of June 30, 2015.

Ivy League colleges

Brown University
www.brown.edu
Providence, RI

Columbia University
www.columbia.edu
New York City, NY

Cornell University
www.cornell.edu
Ithaca, NY

Dartmouth College
www.dartmouth.edu
Hanover, NH

Harvard University
www.harvard.edu
Cambridge, MA

Princeton University
www.princeton.edu
Princeton, NJ

University of Pennsylvania
www.upenn.edu
Philadelphia, PA

Yale University
www.yale.edu
New Haven, CT

Ivy League schools tend to rank high on various world rankings of universities; however, they are not leaders in all subject areas. If you are thinking about applying to an "Ivy League" school because of its reputation, make sure to research which subjects it excels at.

It helps to keep in mind that "Ivy League" schools are not large institutions. Their student bodies range from 4,000 to 13,000 students, which puts them in the small- to mid-range category for American post-secondary institutions. The eight "Ivy League" schools are listed on the previous page. Their respective locations and approximate student bodies are also listed.

PUBLIC COLLEGES

In contrast to private colleges, there are more than 1,500 public colleges across the United States. Public colleges include some of the largest university campuses in the United States.

Public colleges and universities cater to students emerging from a broad range of socio-economic backgrounds. They offer a wide range of degrees and, generally speaking, they are more multi-cultural and linguistically diverse environments compared to their private school counterparts.

Publicly-funded and publicly-supported colleges can be found in every state in the U.S. (including Hawaii and Alaska). Some examples include the institutions noted in the box to the right. Note; mega-universities, such as the University of California, have multiple state wide campuses. Each campus is considered to be a separate university, even though funding for the entire series of campuses stems from the same government source (i.e. the State of California).

Public Colleges

University of California—Berkeley
www.berkeley.edu
Berkeley, CA

University of California—Los Angeles
www.ucla.edu
Los Angeles, CA

University of Virginia
www.virginia.edu
Charlottesville, VA

University of Michigan—Ann Arbor
www.umich.edu
Ann Arbor, MI

University of North Carolina
www.unc.edu
Chapel Hill, NC

College of William and Mary
www.wm.edu
Williamsburg, VA

Georgia Institute of Technology
www.gatech.edu
Atlanta, Georgia

University of Washington
www.washington.edu
Seattle, WA

University of Texas
www.utexas.edu
Austin, TX

Pennsylvania State University—
University Park
www.psu.edu
University Park, PA

Liberal Arts colleges

Oftentimes you will see references to "liberal arts colleges." These institutions are like any other public or private college, except for one thing—they focus solely on the "liberal arts."

You will not find technical degrees, such as; engineering, medicine, nursing, or business at most of these highly specialised colleges. The content of a "liberal arts" degree is open to debate. The various liberal arts colleges provide widely varying curriculum programs.

The overall aim of a liberal arts college is to provide students with a broad education, in various fields, in the hopes of producing better, more reasoned thinkers. To put it bluntly, liberal arts colleges want to train you to think "outside the box" on a variety of historical, political, sociological, mathematical, and scientific issues.

The idea underpinning the college philosophy is that undergraduate degrees should provide students with an education in world affairs and global humanity. Only after gaining such, broad-based, knowledge should a student aim to pursue a specific technical degree, such as; medicine, engineering, or any other vocational training program.

There are many highly successful liberal arts colleges in the United States and they have formed a well-organized community of national and state-level schools. Such colleges, generally, have small student bodies and they often boast high teacher-to-student ratios.

Liberal arts colleges

Amherst College
www.amherst.edu
Amherst, MA

Carleton College
www.carleton.edu
Northfield, MI

Grinnell College
www.grinnell.edu
Grinnell, IA

Haverford College
www.haverford.edu
Haverford, PA

Middlebury College
www.middlebury.edu
Middlebury, VT

Williams College
www.williams.edu
Williamstown, MA

Bowdoin College
www.bowdoin.edu
Brunswick, ME

For more information visit
www.collegenews.org

Many liberal arts colleges cater to specific communities, including; Aboriginal, African-American, religious, women-only, and men-only communities. Some well-known examples of liberal arts colleges in the U.S. include; but are not limited to, those listed in the box to the right.

Community colleges

Community colleges serve two primary purposes:

(1) To serve as a bridge between high school and college, by providing students with transition courses that transfer into four-year Bachelor of Arts (B.A) and Bachelor of Science (B.Sc.) degrees.
Approximately two out of every five American students start their university careers in this way. Community colleges also offer a range of four-year degree programs, are nationally recognized degrees, and are accessible to students who are restricted to particular geographic locations.

(2) To prepare students for jobs right away, by offering; entry-level career training, vocational training, and adult upgrading.
Such programs are usually completed in the form of a two-year diploma program.

Community colleges

Atlanta Technical College, GA
www.atlantatech.edu

Cascadia Community College, WA
www.cascadia.edu

Southern University at Shreveport, LA
www.web.susla.edu

Southwestern Community college, NC
www.southwesterncc.edu

North Florida Community College, FL
www.nfcc.edu

Texas State Technical College, TX
www.tstc.edu

Community colleges are less expensive places to study compared to mainstream colleges. They are often publicly-funded and their overhead costs, are usually, much less than those of larger colleges. If you are tight on finances, but you still want to start working towards your degree, a community college might be the right place for you. Courses at community colleges are accredited university-level courses, they go towards the requirements of your overall degree. You will end up paying much less, for the same education, than you would pay had you entered a mainstream college right out of high school.

Community colleges can offer you more choice in location and course options. There are over 1200 community colleges across the United States and they all benefit from articulation agreements that exist with local mainstream colleges.

Often times college ranking systems ignore community colleges entirely. This is partly due to the fact that many students who start their studies at a community college do not graduate from that college. Rather, after a year or two, they move on to larger colleges. This mobility is an indication of the successful procedures that exist between many community and mainstream colleges.

Most community colleges have student bodies ranging between 1,000 and 3,000. However, there are some community colleges that can boast student populations of more than 4,000.

For student surveys, recounting the benefits of particular community institutions consider the following site: www.ccsse.org.

DEFINING TERMS

Now that you have learned to categorize and define the various types of colleges in the U.S., it is useful for you to learn their lingo as well.

There are a number of references specific to American college life that are not reflected in our British- and French-inspired Canadian university system.

Be prepared for the following terms:

American term	Canadian equivalent
"college"	university
"dormitory"	residence
"college catalogue"	course calendar *(a listing of all courses and their descriptions)*
"view book"	university handbook *(a brief guide to the university, including campus maps and student services)*
"freshman"	first-year student
"sophomore"	second-year student
"junior"	third-year student
"senior"	fourth-year or honours student
"GPA"	Grade Point Average

ADMISSIONS

Navigating through university websites can be a nightmare.

In recent years, colleges have pumped a lot of money into their websites so you can easily find the admissions information. It is also possible, and even expected that you use the university's website to; apply, for entry, pay fees, and communicate with university staff and admissions officers. That said, some colleges have websites that are much more user-friendly than others.

Throughout your application journey, the section of a college's website that will be of most interest to you is its "Admissions" page. On some college sites, "Admissions" appears as a direct link from the home page. On other college sites, you first have to click to enter one of the following sections (or a version thereof): potential students, applying students, high school students, or applicants.

The more you navigate through different college websites the more you'll get used to, quickly finding the admissions section.

The admissions department in every college is responsible for processing your application and ensuring you meet the college's basic requirements, before passing your application to a particular department for further analysis. Admissions departments are also responsible for disseminating scholarships and awards. This is because many scholarships and awards are based on your initial admissions application.

If you want to know about the specific requirements you must meet in order to gain entry to any college, find that college's admissions website and look for its "entrance requirements" or "application requirements" section.

The entrance/application requirements pages always indicate the basic requirements for entry to your college of choice, including the following:

- the average high school grade (or GPA equivalent) of successful applicants
- the number of letters of reference required for application
- the application deadline
- the average SAT/ACT score range among successful applicants
- the need for SAT Subject Tests (or specific SAT Subject Tests)
- any other specific requirements for particular departments or degree programs

A successful application is dependent on many factors. One of which is, the applicant must supply all correct information as stipulated by the College's admission office. Make sure you understand what the college is asking of you, before you submit your application, and if you're at all unsure, or you want confirmation that what you are thinking is in fact correct, then contact the college's admissions staff.

It's their job to help you!

Each college's admissions website will provide you with contact information for your queries and concerns.

Use that information!

Each college employs full-time staffers, whose job it is to answer your admissions questions.

ADMISSIONS CASE STUDY

Each college is unique in terms of how it runs its application and admissions procedures.

On the next few pages, you will find an example of the college admissions website at Princeton University.

PRINCETON UNIVERSITY

The appearance of the pages that follow will change over time as the university updates its website.

Admission and Aid: Princeton

Go to Princeton's main page located at www.princeton.edu

You will see, in the left-hand column, a direct link to **Admission and Aid.**

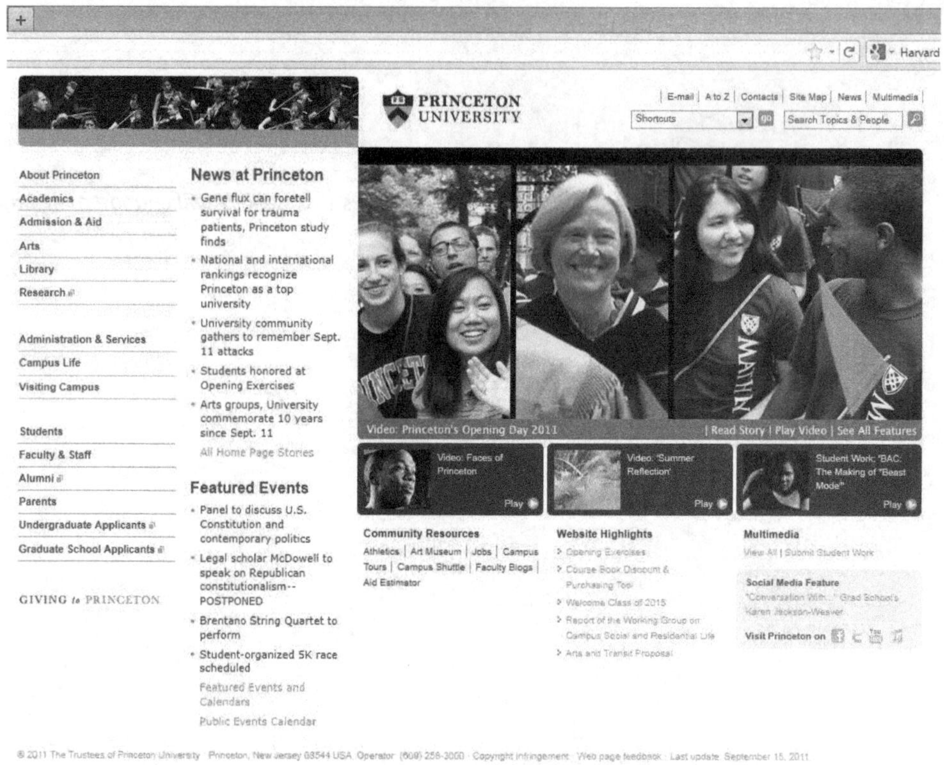

Click on the college's **Admission and Aid** link, which takes you to the following page: www.princeton.edu/main/admission-aid

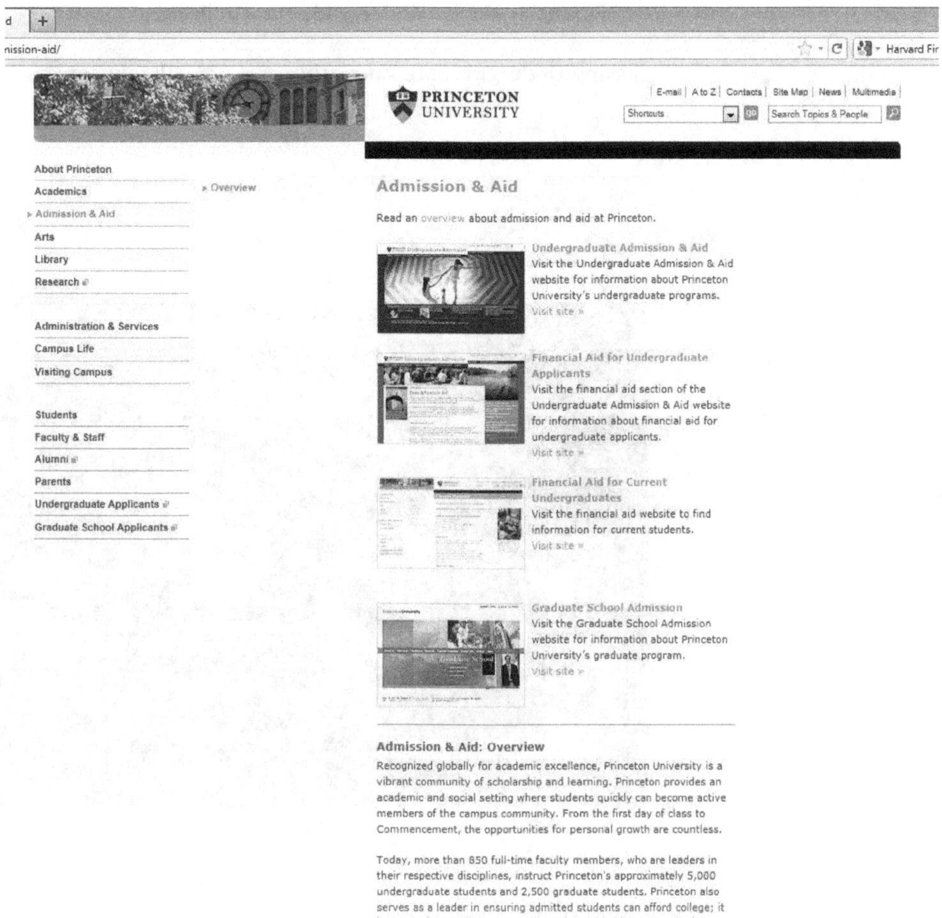

UNDERGRADUATE ADMISSION AND AID: PRINCETON

Take some time to look through the sections on this page.

The two links, of most importance to you, will be **Undergraduate Admission and Aid** and **Financial Aid for Undergraduate Applicants**.

Clicking **Undergraduate Admission and Aid** will take you to the following site.

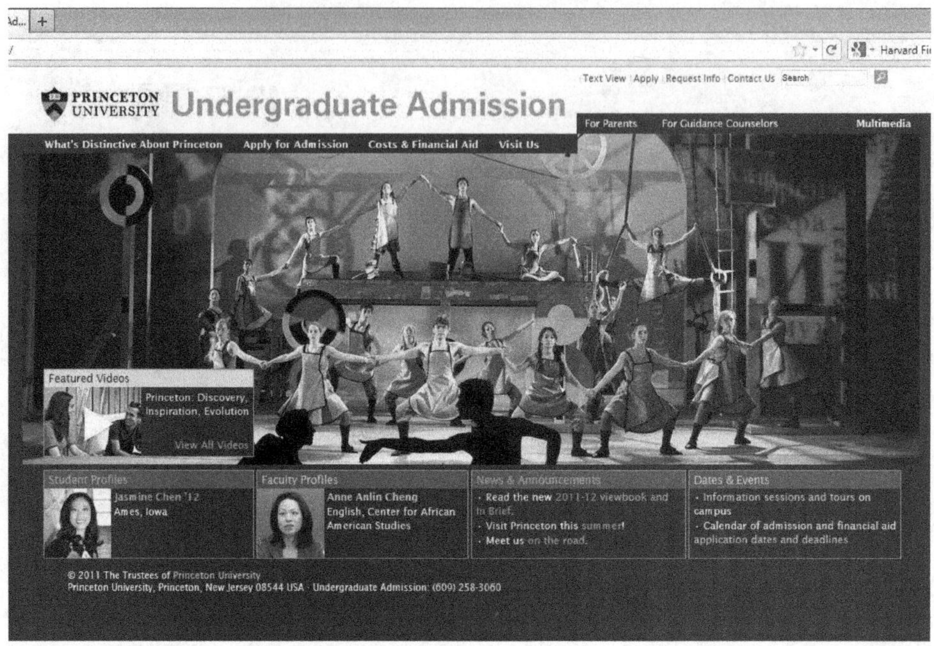

Apply for Admission: Princeton

Here you will see **Apply for Admission** at the top of the page.

Clicking on that link will take you to the university's application website,

http://admission.princeton.edu/applyingforadmission

Applying for Admission |

admission.princeton.edu/applyingforadmission

PRINCETON UNIVERSITY Undergraduate Admission

Apply | Request Info | Contact Us

What's Distinctive About Princeton | Apply for Admission | Costs & Financial Aid | Visit Us | For Parents | For Guidance Counselors | Video | Blog

Chang-rae Lee

Certificate Programs

Angela Cai '09, alumna

Home » Applying for Admission

Applying for Admission

Princeton's admission process goes beyond simply looking for academically accomplished students. For each freshman class, we bring together a varied mix of high-achieving, intellectually gifted students from diverse backgrounds to create an exceptional learning community. We care about what students have accomplished in and out of the classroom. The process is highly selective. In recent years, we've offered admission to less than 10 percent of applicants.

As you prepare your application, help us to appreciate your talents, academic accomplishments and personal achievements. We'll ask for your transcript and recommendations, and we will want to know more than just the statistics in your file. Tell us your story. Show us what's special about you. Tell us how you would seize the academic and non-academic opportunities at Princeton and contribute to the Princeton community. Above all, please write in a style that reflects your own voice.

How to Apply

Princeton accepts the Common Application and the Universal College Application. Princeton treats them both equally. To apply using the Common Application, you will need to submit both the Common Application and Princeton's writing supplement to the Common Application through the Common Application website. Although applying online is preferred, you also may apply by paper. A PDF of the application is available, as well as a PDF of Princeton's writing supplement to the Common Application.

To apply online using the Universal College Application, please visit the Universal College Application website, where you will find the First-Year Admissions Application and Princeton Supplement to the Universal College Application. If you prefer to apply by paper, a PDF of the application is available on the Universal College Application website, as well as a PDF of the Princeton Supplement to the Universal College Application.

When to Apply

You have two choices for applying to Princeton -- single-choice early action or regular decision. Before you begin preparing your application, we strongly encourage you to review our publication Ready Set Go (.pdf), which contains detailed information regarding Princeton's application process, standardized testing

Application Requirements

Single-Choice Early Action

Standardized Testing

Academic Preparation

Helpful Tips

Application Dates & Deadlines

Admission Statistics

Admission FAQ

Tips for Home Schooled Students

Tips for International Students

Apply Now

Request Information

Joint Ivy Statement on Admission Policies

Contact Us

Related Links:

Academic Departments & Programs

The Common Application

The Universal College Application

WAYS TO APPLY: PRINCETON

You will see that Princeton provides information on the various means of applying. Note: there is usually more than one way to apply!

You should choose one application approach and stick to it.

PREPSKILLS® recommends students apply online.

Online applications cause fewer headaches. You won't have to worry about whether the application will arrive on time, whether it will get lost in the post, whether it will arrive squished and crumpled, or whether you've put enough stamps on the envelope to ensure timely delivery.

With online applications, you can (and always should) print out various draft copies to edit, with a red pen, before submitting the final version, via Internet.

Dates and Deadlines: Princeton

On the university's application website (http://admission.princeton.edu/applyingforadmission) click on **Application Dates & Deadlines** in the right-hand side bar. You will arrive at the following website: https://admission.princeton.edu/applyingforadmission/application-dates-deadlines

Consult the **Dates and Deadlines** section of the admissions page to determine when the particular portions of your application are due. If you are planning to apply using the college's **paper application**, you must determine whether the deadline for submission is the **postmark date**, or the **arrival date**, of the package.

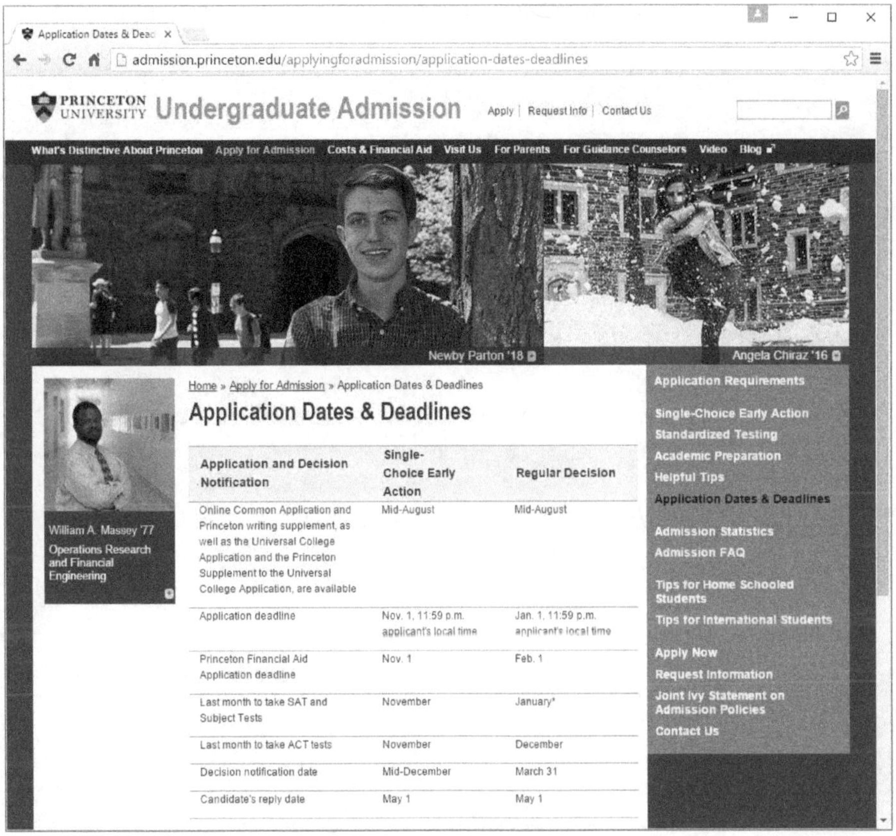

Application and Decision Notification	Single-Choice Early Action	Regular Decision
Online Common Application and Princeton writing supplement, as well as the Universal College Application and the Princeton Supplement to the Universal College Application, are available	Mid-August	Mid-August
Application deadline	Nov. 1, 11:59 p.m. applicant's local time	Jan. 1, 11:59 p.m. applicant's local time
Princeton Financial Aid Application deadline	Nov. 1	Feb. 1
Last month to take SAT and Subject Tests	November	January*
Last month to take ACT tests	November	December
Decision notification date	Mid-December	March 31
Candidate's reply date	May 1	May 1

This site provides you with an outline of all application due dates.

Disclaimer:
Please note the images provided here are samples only.
ALWAYS check with the college's Admission Department for up-to-date application due dates.

The **Dates and Deadlines**, website also provides you with links to the application forms, as well as specific deadlines related to standardized tests.

Required Tests - PRINCETON

Standardized Testing

To be considered for admission to Princeton, you must submit the results of the SAT Reasoning Test or ACT (with Writing, where offered). In addition, all applicants must submit the results of two different SAT Subject Tests. Princeton does not use minimum cutoff scores for standardized tests in their admission decisions.

Required Tests

When applying for admission to Princeton, you must submit official scores for either the SAT Reasoning Test or the ACT (with Writing, where available). All applicants must also take two SAT Subject Tests.

Applicants who intend to pursue a B.S.E. degree should take one SAT Subject Test in either physics or chemistry and one SAT Subject Test in mathematics (Level I or II).

If you choose to take more than two subject tests, we will consider all your scores, giving the greatest weight to your two strongest scores.

www.princeton.edu/admission/applyingforadmission/standardized_testing

PREPSKILLS® Disclaimer: Please note the information provided here is a sample only. ALWAYS check with the college's Admission Department for up-to-date application requirements.

ADMISSIONS STATISTICS: PRINCETON

The vast majority of colleges will provide admissions statistics. Sometimes this information is found under the "college profile" or "university profile."

Below is an example taken from Princeton University's entrance and admissions statistics for the graduating class of 2019 (entrants for 2015).

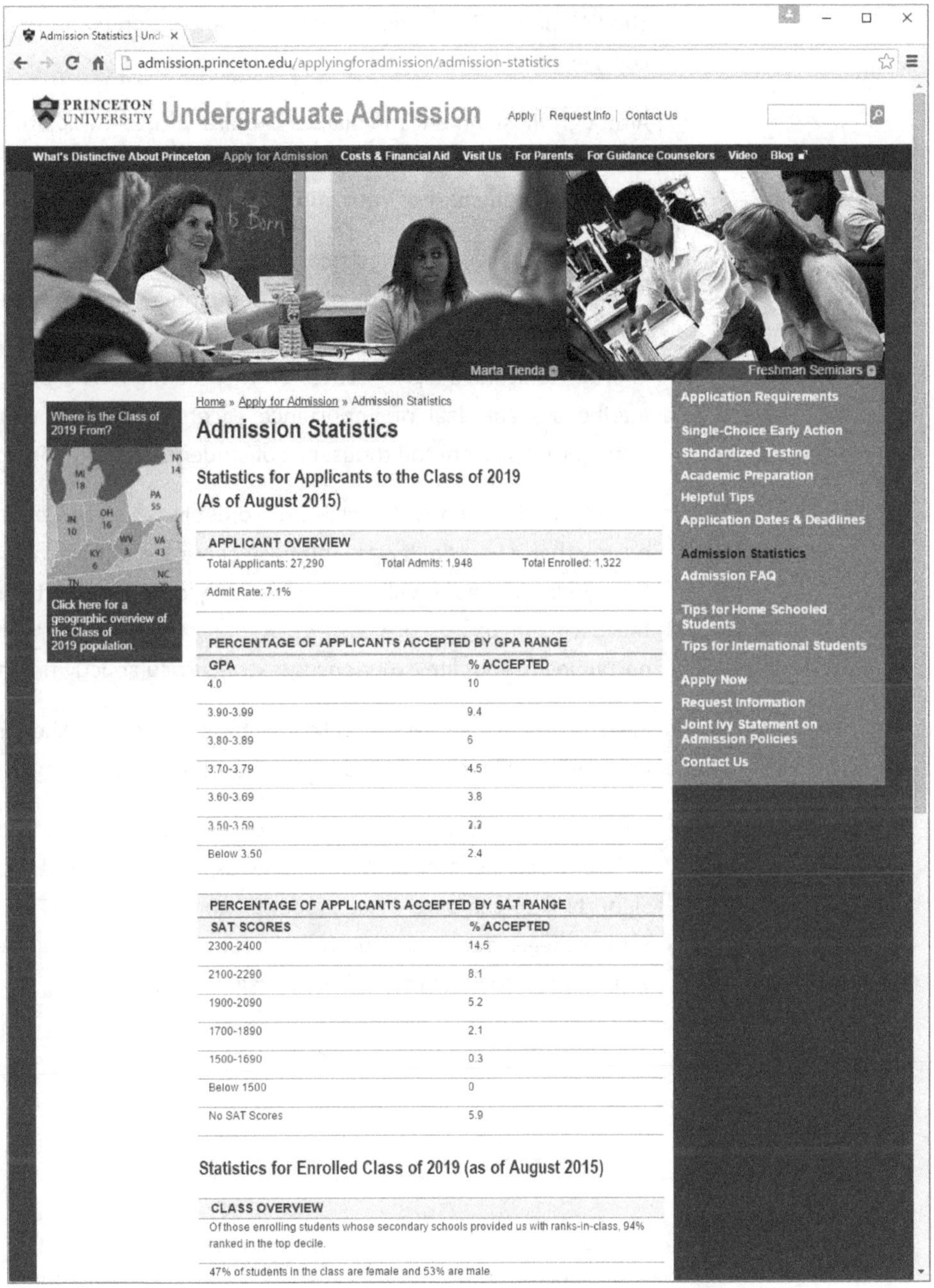
Admission Statistics | Und

admission.princeton.edu/applyingforadmission/admission-statistics

PRINCETON UNIVERSITY Undergraduate Admission

Apply | Request Info | Contact Us

What's Distinctive About Princeton | Apply for Admission | Costs & Financial Aid | Visit Us | For Parents | For Guidance Counselors | Video | Blog

Marta Tienda

Freshman Seminars

Where is the Class of 2019 From?

Click here for a geographic overview of the Class of 2019 population.

Home » Apply for Admission » Admission Statistics

Admission Statistics

Statistics for Applicants to the Class of 2019 (As of August 2015)

APPLICANT OVERVIEW

Total Applicants: 27,290 | Total Admits: 1,948 | Total Enrolled: 1,322

Admit Rate: 7.1%

PERCENTAGE OF APPLICANTS ACCEPTED BY GPA RANGE

GPA	% ACCEPTED
4.0	10
3.90-3.99	9.4
3.80-3.89	6
3.70-3.79	4.5
3.60-3.69	3.8
3.50-3.59	3.3
Below 3.50	2.4

PERCENTAGE OF APPLICANTS ACCEPTED BY SAT RANGE

SAT SCORES	% ACCEPTED
2300-2400	14.5
2100-2290	8.1
1900-2090	5.2
1700-1890	2.1
1500-1690	0.3
Below 1500	0
No SAT Scores	5.9

Statistics for Enrolled Class of 2019 (as of August 2015)

CLASS OVERVIEW

Of those enrolling students whose secondary schools provided us with ranks-in-class, 94% ranked in the top decile.

47% of students in the class are female and 53% are male.

Application Requirements
Single-Choice Early Action
Standardized Testing
Academic Preparation
Helpful Tips
Application Dates & Deadlines
Admission Statistics
Admission FAQ
Tips for Home Schooled Students
Tips for International Students
Apply Now
Request Information
Joint Ivy Statement on Admission Policies
Contact Us

http://admission.princeton.edu/applyingforadmission/admission-statistics

STANDARDIZED TESTING

SAT VERSUS ACT

The SAT and ACT are two standard entrance examinations. They are used by American colleges to rank applicants.

Although most American colleges require you to complete either the SAT or the ACT (most colleges allow you to choose which one you want to complete), your score on that exam is only **one part of your application.**

Even if you achieve a perfect score on your SAT or ACT exam, it does not guarantee you entrance to your preferred college. Remember, lots of students will use extra tutoring and complete special training courses (such as the PREPSKILLS® SAT and ACT programs) in order to achieve higher scores on their admissions exams. This means most colleges ascribe a great deal of importance to other parts of your application in order to distinguish you from the thousands of students that send in applications every year.

In fact, the SAT and ACT scores are sometimes used as bare minimum standards. This means that if you don't pass the **base score** set out by the college you are applying to then your application will be automatically dropped. Increasingly, colleges are avoiding the use of a base score system. Rather, they are trying to integrate other factors pertaining to your life experiences, extra-curricular activities, and reference letters.

Even if you do surpass a college's base score, it's the first step. After that, your application will be judged based on your other qualifications.

Because the SAT and ACT are different types of standardized tests, they produce different scoring scales. Many colleges, in the United States, employ equivalency algorithms to compare those students who write the SAT to those who write the ACT. Some colleges may state a preference for one test over another. If this is the case, it is in your interest to write the test the college prefers.

WHICH TEST IS MORE POPULAR: SAT OR ACT?

According to college admissions statistics for 2013, an overwhelming percentage of students submit SAT scores. All of the Ivy League schools, as well as the largest state universities (such as the University of California), and most liberal arts colleges (such as Washington College), report more than 90 percent of their applicants submitted SAT scores. By comparison, those same universities reported only 15 to 30 percent of their applicants submitted ACT scores (Amherst is a notable exception, where over 70 percent of applicants submitted ACT scores).

There is overlap in these numbers as many students have submitted scores for ***both*** exams. If you are one of those students, the college will consider both scores as part of your application.

The **SAT** is the **more popular** exam to write. According to analysts this is because the SAT is "easier" to prepare for in a shorter period of time, while the ACT requires more profound knowledge skills.

It may be for this reason that many students prefer the SAT to the ACT, and it is a consideration you should take into account if you are pressed for time.

Whether you decide to write the SAT, the ACT, or both, a training course will improve your scores! For more information, visit www.prepskills.com

PSAT: STANDARDIZED TESTING IN GRADE 10

Many students wait until Grade 11, or even Grade 12, before they start to think about the SAT and ACT. Waiting can jeopardize your chances at US college enrollment, so starting as early as Grade 9 or 10 is ideal.

The PSAT is an excellent way to do that. Writing the PSAT provides you with a number of informative and financially-rewarding possibilities.

The PSAT officially stands for **Preliminary SAT**. It also goes by the name, **National Merit Scholarship Qualifying Test** (or NMSQT) and it is co-sponsored by the College Board and the National Merit Scholarship Corporation (NMSC).

To find out more about the PSAT/NMSQT visit:
https://collegereadiness.collegeboard.org/psat-nmsqt-psat-10

WHAT DOES THE PSAT TEST?

As you might have guessed, the PSAT is a mini-version of the SAT. It's written by students in grades 10 and 11. It does not include higher-level algebra questions. The vocabulary, while difficult, is slightly simpler than the vocabulary that you will find on the SAT.

There is a great deal of overlap between the PSAT and the SAT. Writing the PSAT will prepare you for the SAT in terms of content. It will also give you a sense of where your scoring range is. This can help you determine how much extra SAT training you'll need in order to achieve the final SAT score you want (or need) to present in your college application.

The PSAT/NMSQT measures the following skills:

- critical reading
- math problem-solving
- writing

PSAT/NMSQT STRUCTURE

The PSAT/NMSQT includes five sections. It takes a total of 2 hours and 45 minutes to complete.

Section	Format	Content
Reading	60-minute reading section	47 critical reading questions
Writing and Language	35-minute section	44 writing questions for improving sentence/paragraph structure, diction, grammar, and expression of ideas
Mathematics (No Calculator)	25-minute section	17 questions
Mathematics (Calculator)	45-minute section	31 questions

When should I write the PSAT?

The College Board (jointly with the National Merit Scholarship) writes and administers the PSAT once a year in October.

In Canada, the PSAT is offered and administered by individual high schools. Your school may, or may not, offer the PSAT. If it does not offer the PSAT, you can register at a private or public high school that does offer the exam.

Parents must register their children with high schools directly. Your local school board can help you identify schools in your area offer the PSAT. Alternatively, you can contact PREPSKILLS for information about high schools offering the PSAT in the Greater Toronto Area and Ottawa.

You will find information related to the PSAT on the College Board website www.collegeboard.org.

Students should enroll in a training course to maximize their PSAT potential!

Contact PREPSKILLS® for more information or to register for its annual PREPSKILLS® PSAT Preparation Course, which is offered in August/September of each year.

WHY TAKE THE PSAT?

The PSAT is a practice run for the real SAT. It is also good practice for those students who are thinking about writing the ACT. Students will find their final SAT and ACT scores improve if they have prepared for, and written, the PSAT.

There are other tangible benefits to writing the PSAT. If you are an American citizen, as well as a Canadian citizen (e.g. if one of your parents is American and you have dual-citizenship), a high PSAT score may qualify you for a National Merit Scholarship (administered by the National Merit Scholarship Corporation), a National Hispanic Recognition scholarship (administered by the National Hispanic Program), or a Telluride Association scholarship (for gifted juniors planning to attend summer seminars in the humanities).

If you are not an American citizen, writing the PSAT will still serve as a gateway to college. Colleges often begin to recruit students based on PSAT performance. Those students who perform well on the PSAT are put onto a national list of top-ranking PSAT scorers. That list is then passed on to colleges and universities across the country. Based on your scores, colleges and universities will send you information on scholarships and awards, application materials, recruitment materials, and the school's programs and campus life. That information can prove crucial in helping you decide which college, or university, you ultimately apply to.

You should use the PSAT opportunity to put yourself on the admissions radar screen. To do so, make sure to select "Yes" under "Student Search Service" when you write your PSAT. That is the service colleges and universities use to identify test-takers they wish to recruit. Within a few months, you may find you are receiving information pamphlets, and other helpful information, from colleges.

For more information, visit:

www.collegereadiness.collegeboard.org/psat-nmsqt-psat-10

THE SAT REASONING TEST

In the past, the SAT stood for Scholastic Aptitude Test or Scholastic Assessment Test. The acronym no longer stands for anything in particular, the test simply goes by the full title of, SAT Reasoning Test.

In order to write the SAT, students must go to **www.collegeboard.org** and register for a particular sitting.

There are specific test dates for the SAT, at **Canadian testing centres**. To guarantee a place at one of those centres, on a specific date, you must register weeks in advance. There is a fee for registering (which is updated each year), you must pay the registration fee, online, before you are allowed to write the exam. The College Board website will describe the various testing locations in your geographical area.

The SAT test is composed of four components:

- evidence-based reading
- writing and language
- mathematics
- essay (optional)

Reading Test One section of 65 minutes

This section includes 4 single passages and 1 paired passage. These readings include 1 passage in U.S. and World Literature, 2 passages in History/Social Studies, and 2 passages in Science, all of which are followed by reading comprehension questions. Two passages (1 Science passage and 1 History/Social Studies passage) will also include graphics.

Writing and Language Test One section of 35 minutes

This section includes 4 passages, one each from Careers, History/Social Studies, Humanities, and Science. It includes questions that test your skills in expressing ideas and using Standard English Conventions.

Mathematics Two sections totaling 80 minutes

There is 1 calculator section and 1 non-calculator section. The Mathematics section includes questions in number theory, word problems, geometry (including trigonometry), basic algebra and higher-level algebra, including quadratic equations.

Essay One optional section of 50 minutes

This section will require you to respond to a source text while considering the author's usage of evidence, reasoning, and stylistic elements. This section is optional, but is required by some universities and programs.

SAT SURVIVAL TIPS

1. It will not help much if you wait to finish Grade 12 courses before writing the SAT. The exam is composed of mathematical, reading, and writing content you learn from **Grade 6** to **Grade 11**.

2. **Practice, practice, practice**! The more you practice with SAT-style problems, the better you will do.

3. Make sure to use up-to-date SAT examples in your preparations. The SAT has gone through many revisions and reforms. Past exam and preparation books are out-of-date and do not reflect current SAT content.

4. On the test day, arrive early and make sure to bring your registration ticket, extra pencils (and a sharpener), and snacks for the breaks (including a bottle of water).

5. New reforms to the SAT scoring system mean that you can choose which scores to send to colleges, this is called Score Choice.

WRITING A SUCCESSFUL SAT ESSAY

1. **Never use a pen!** You will score zero if you do.

2. Always try to fill both sheets of paper provided to you.

3. Always include an identifiable introduction (with a thesis statement), a body (composed of at least two paragraphs), and an identifiable conclusion (where you sum up your argument).

4. Remember, you will be analyzing the ways in which the author of a given text supports their argument regardless of your personal opinion on the topic!

WHEN THE SAT IS OFFERED

For the 2017-2018 academic year, the SAT will be offered to Canadian test-takers in October, December, March, and May.

SAT SUBJECT TESTS

Although you can often choose to do the SAT Reasoning Test or the ACT College Test, many universities will stipulate that you must also write certain **SAT Subject Tests**.

SAT Subject Tests are standardized tests focusing on particular subject areas, such as; mathematics, physics, chemistry, history, and languages. Depending on the undergraduate program you choose to pursue, the Subject Tests required for your entrance application will vary. Some colleges allow students to choose which SAT Subject Tests they prefer to take, while others stipulate that certain tests are required.

SAT Subject Test scores help you to demonstrate your achievements more generally. Even though many colleges do not require SAT Subject Tests, the admissions department will take scores into account if you have them. This is a tool colleges use to learn more about your academic background. It is an option you should pursue, if you hope to distinguish yourself in the college admissions process.

Contact PREPSKILLS® for specific year-round training programs for the SAT Subject Tests!

SAT Subject Tests

Mathematics
Mathematics Level I
Mathematics Level II

Science
Biology E/M
Chemistry
Physics

Humanities
(English) Literature
U.S. History
World History

Languages
French
French with Listening
German
German with Listening
Spanish
Spanish with Listening
Italian
Modern Hebrew
Japanese with Listening
Chinese with Listening
Korean with Listening
Latin

https://collegereadiness.collegeboard.org/sat-subject-tests/subjects

PLAN YOUR SAT SUBJECT TESTS ONE YEAR IN ADVANCE!

Some colleges require **three SAT Subject Tests** for general entry. Since you cannot write the SAT Reasoning Test the same day you write a SAT Subject Test, you need to plan ahead.

There are a certain number of SAT Subject Test dates throughout the year. Some SAT Subject Tests are available once a year, others are only at American testing sites.

To avoid disappointment, or missed deadlines, consult the SAT Subject Test website: www.collegeboard.org. Always make sure to register early to ensure you have a spot on the particular testing day you want.

The best time to start thinking about the SAT Subject Tests is near the end of Grade 10!

If you are already in Grade 11, don't panic. You still have time to finish all of the tests by Grade 12. But, you need to get moving and start making decisions!

If you are in Grade 12, you may have to limit your choice of colleges and universities, depending on how many SAT Subject Tests they require. There may not be enough time to fit in all the tests required by some colleges before the application deadline (which is usually in November for early action/early decision and in January, or February, for regular enrolment).

The list to the right indicates some of the colleges that require at least two or three SAT Subject Tests (always check the college website to determine the most up-to-date information). This is not a comprehensive list. Make sure you determine how many, if any, SAT Subject Tests are required, by your particular college, by consulting its Admissions website.

College SAT Subject Test Requirements

Colleges that require three SAT Subject Tests

Georgetown University
King's College of London

Colleges that require/recommend two SAT Subject Tests

Amherst College
Barnard College
Brown University
California Institute of Technology
Carnegie Mellon University
Columbia University
Cornell University
Dartmouth College
Davidson College
Duke University
Harvard University
Harvey Mudd College
Haverford College
Massachusetts Institute of Technology
McGill University
Northwestern University
Princeton University
Rice University
Tufts University
University of California, Berkeley
University of California, Irvine
University of California, Los Angeles
University of California, Riverside
University of California, San Diego
University of Pennsylvania
Vassar College
Washington and Lee University
Webb Institute
Wellesley College
Williams College

This is not a comprehensive list. Colleges will consider more than 2 SAT Subject Tests if you submit them. ALWAYS check the college's website for updates.

SAT SCORING

Both the SAT and the ACT base their scoring off scaled models. That means there is no direct arithmetic link between your raw score and your overall scaled score—i.e. the score colleges use to rank you against other applicants. Of course, a greater number of correct answers, and fewer incorrect ones, will always result in a higher scaled score overall, on either exam. However, those scores will be calibrated according to how everyone else in your test session performed on the exam. Your **scaled score** will reflect how well you fared compared to all the other test takers. Your scaled score is actually a ranking that tells you where you place compared to your peers.

The SAT is divided into five sections:

- Reading Test
- Writing and Language Test
- Math Test - No Calculator
- Mathematics - Calculator
- Essay (optional)

The highest possible total score is 1600.

Colleges that focus on academic performance as a key element in their admissions requirements will often indicate a range, between **1900** and **2200,** (i.e. between 630 and 740 per section) is as an average SAT score, among successful applicants. This is for the old SAT, as it has changed for March 2016 onward.

Particular departments within colleges may stipulate specific minimum scores in any one of the sections. For example, if you are applying to mathematics, engineering, chemistry, or physics, you should determine whether the college, or department you are hoping to gain admission to, has stated minimums for the mathematics section of the SAT.

The same holds true for liberal arts degrees. Some college departments, such as; English literature, linguistics, history, or anthropology, might specify minimum scores in the critical reading and writing sections. Interdisciplinary departments, such as; political science, economics, sociology, and history of science, might stipulate minimum scores in all three sections.

On the next page, you will find an example of a SAT score report for tests taken before March 2016.

CollegeBoard SAT

MY SAT ONLINE SCORE REPORT

SAT REASONING TEST JUNE 2008

NOT AN OFFICIAL SCORE REPORT

Summary of Results

Congratulations on taking the SAT Reasoning Test!

You're showing colleges that you are serious about getting an education. The SAT is one indicator of how ready you are to handle college-level work. The test measures what you learned in high school and how well you can apply that knowledge. Both skills are essential to doing well in high school and in college.

CRITICAL READING: **640**

RANGE 200 – 800: 610 - 670

When you take tests more than once, your scores may vary. This expected variation is considered your score range.

National Percentile: 88%

	TOTAL QUESTIONS	CORRECT ANSWERS	INCORRECT ANSWERS	OMITTED ANSWERS
CRITICAL READING				
SENTENCE COMPLETION	19	12	4	3
PASSAGE-BASED READING	48	41	[illegible]	0
TOTAL	[illegible]	53	[illegible]	3

See page 3 for details on your critical reading score.

MATHEMATICS: **710**

RANGE 200 – 800

When you take tests more than once, your scores may vary. This expected variation is considered your score range.

National Percentile: [illegible]

	TOTAL QUESTIONS	CORRECT ANSWERS	INCORRECT ANSWERS	OMITTED ANSWERS
MATHEMATICS				
NUMBER AND OPERATIONS	12	10	1	1
ALGEBRA AND FUNCTIONS	20	19	0	1
GEOMETRY AND MEASUREMENT	15	15	0	0
DATA ANALYSIS, STATISTICS, AND PROBABILITY	7	5	2	0
TOTAL	54	49	3	2

See page 4 for details on your mathematics score.

SAMPLE

WRITING: **73[illegible]**

RANGE 200 – 800: 690 - 770

When you take tests more than once, your scores may vary. This expected variation is considered your score range.

National Percentile: 98%

	TOTAL QUESTIONS	CORRECT ANSWERS	INCORRECT ANSWERS	OMITTED ANSWERS
WRITING				
IMPROVING SENTENCES	25	23	2	0
IDENTIFYING SENTENCE ERRORS	18	17	1	0
IMPROVING PARAGRAPHS	6	6	0	0
MULTIPLE CHOICE TOTAL	49	46	3	0

ESSAY: 8

See page 5 for details on your writing score.
On page 6, view the essay you wrote.

See Glossary of Terms on page 10

A printout of this page will **not** be accepted by colleges as an official score report.

Score Choice

In the past, students had to submit all their SAT scores to their chosen colleges. That meant that if you wrote the test three times, all three sets of scores would be forwarded to your college(s) of choice.

New changes to the SAT reporting rules mean that students can now pick which scores to send to their college(s) of choice. The aim of this new rule, known as Score Choice, is to decrease stress on student applicants. Unfortunately, it also means many students will now likely opt to rewrite the SAT a number of times, knowing that not all scores will be forwarded to the colleges. As a result of the new changes, students will likely fall into the trap of paying to take the exam repeatedly, without improving upon their overall ranking.

Research has consistently shown the SAT and ACT tests are designed so you perform within the same narrow score band each time you write the test, unless you changed your study habits by taking additional training courses in between testing sessions. In other words, writing the test repeatedly will not improve your score, unless you take training courses that provide you with exposure to SAT or ACT style questions.

The PREPSKILLS® philosophy is *DO IT ONCE, DO IT RIGHT!*

Avoid rewriting the test multiple times. Not only is it a waste of your time, money, and energy, but it will not change your score much if you fail to undergo specialised training in the interim. It is a much better approach to prepare properly the first time around, and to score high in your first sitting, than to write, and rewrite, the test ad nauseum.

Also, many colleges—including Yale and Stanford—reject Score Choice, which means if you write the exam more than once, you must send all of your scores to the college!

Find out whether your college accepts, or rejects, Score Choice and then contact PREPSKILLS® to find out about our SAT training courses that meet your personal scheduling needs.

When do you get your SAT scores?

The College Board is very specific about when SAT scores get released. Due to the Score Choice changes mentioned on the previous page, students can now view their scores online and pick which scores to send to particular colleges at any given time. However, some colleges ***do not* accept scores via the Internet**, and they will not confirm, or acknowledge, receipt of your scores until they receive the paper copy of your results in the mail.

The table on the next page indicates the score distribution dates for 2015-2016. It is indicative of the manner in which the College Board disseminates scores each year.

Your high school has a **six-digit** SAT School Code.

You will need to record that code when you register for the SAT.

A complete list of high school codes can be found on the College Board website, using the following URL:

www.collegeboard.org/student/testing/sat/codelist.html

It is your responsibility to ensure your scores arrive to your college(s) of choice, on time. It is incumbent upon you to schedule your SAT Reasoning Test with enough time, allowing for your scores to be delivered (usually by post) to the respective institution(s), before the application deadline.

Note that most colleges will accept October and November score reports for their early entrance deadlines. Ensure this is the case with your college, check the colleges admissions website or call the institution directly.

SAMPLE SAT SCORE RELEASE DATES (2015-2016)

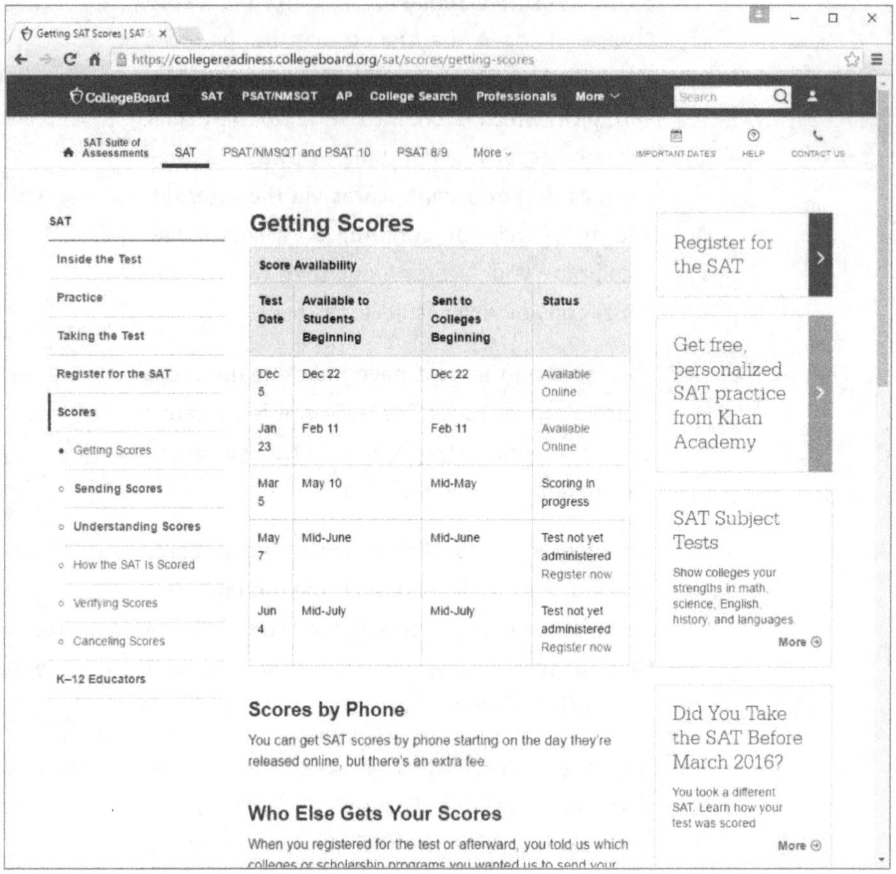

Getting Scores

Score Availability			
Test Date	Available to Students Beginning	Sent to Colleges Beginning	Status
Dec 5	Dec 22	Dec 22	Available Online
Jan 23	Feb 11	Feb 11	Available Online
Mar 5	May 10	Mid-May	Scoring in progress
May 7	Mid-June	Mid-June	Test not yet administered Register now
Jun 4	Mid-July	Mid-July	Test not yet administered Register now

Scores by Phone

You can get SAT scores by phone starting on the day they're released online, but there's an extra fee.

Who Else Gets Your Scores

When you registered for the test or afterward, you told us which

https://collegereadiness.collegeboard.org/sat/scores/getting-scores

THE ACT COLLEGE TEST

The ACT originally stood for **American College Test**. However, nowadays, the non-profit organization that administers the ACT exam refers to it as the **"ACT College Test."**

As with the SAT, there are specific test dates for the ACT. To ensure your place at one of those testing sessions, students are advised to register months in advance. You can do so by going to:

http://www.act.org/content/act/en/register.html

The ACT is composed of four mandatory sections and one optional section:

- English
- Mathematics
- Reading
- Science
- Writing Test (optional)

The mandatory sections are composed of multiple-choice questions. The ACT puts more focus on specific science topics. If science is a strong point for you, then you may want to consider the ACT.

The ACT also contains an optional Writing component, which is 40 minutes long. The Writing Test is separate from the main part of the ACT exam.

If you decide to take the ACT College Test, you may not have to write the essay section, as not all colleges require it. The ACT website provides a list of all colleges that do require the writing component.

WHEN THE ACT IS OFFERED?

The ACT is offered in September, October, December, February, April, and June.

Contact PREPSKILLS® for year-round training programs for the ACT College Test!

ACT SCORING

The ACT Composite Score is the average of the four mandatory sections (English, Mathematics, Reading, and Science) rounded to the nearest whole number. The highest possible overall score is 36.

The ACT also computes **sub-scores,** which divide each section into mini-sections.

- The English section of the exam is sub-divided into usage/mechanics and rhetorical skills.
- The Mathematics section is subdivided into pre-algebra/elementary algebra, plane geometry/trigonometry, and algebra/coordinate geometry.
- The Reading section is subdivided into social studies/sciences and arts/literature.
- The Science section has no subdivisions.

The top score in any subdivision is **18**. Your sub-scores, in any section, do not always add up to your overall score for that section. The scores are scaled according to overlapping averaging and statistical models.

As of September 2015, the ACT enhanced the optional writing test. It is graded based on four subdivisions:

- Ideas and analysis
- Development and support
- Organization
- Language use and conventions

They are each graded from 2-12 and their total sum is scaled from 1-36 to make up the writing score.

The next page has an example of an ACT score report for September 2015 onward. The table also indicates the sub-scores the student achieved in each section.

The ACT® Student Report

ACT, Inc.—Confidential Restricted when data present

ANN C TAYLOR (ACT ID: -54116290)
WHEAT RIDGE SR HIGH SCHOOL (061-450) | APR 2016 NATIONAL

Composite Score 21 U.S. Rank 56% | State Rank 58%

Test Results	Score	U.S. Rank
English	**24**	**74%**
Usage/Mechanics	12	72%
Rhetorical Skills	12	71%
Mathematics	**19**	**47%**
Pre-Algebra/Elem. Algebra	11	57%
Algebra/Coord. Geometry	10	51%
Plane Geometry/Trig.	09	39%
Reading	**23**	**66%**
Social Studies/Sciences	12	67%
Arts/Literature	11	58%
Science	**18**	**32%**
Writing	**25**	**79%**
Ideas and Analysis	10	
Development and Support	08	
Organization	07	
Language Use and Conventions	08	
ELA	**24**	**70%**
STEM		**40%**

Understanding Complex Texts
Proficient

Progress Toward Career Readiness
You are making progress toward a Gold level on the ACT NCRC.

Composite and Subscores: ACT test scores and the Composite score range from 1 to 36; subscores range from 1 to 18. Your Composite score is the average of your scores on the four subject tests. Subscores do not necessarily add up to your score for a subject test.

ACT College Readiness Benchmarks: If your scores are at or above the ACT benchmark scores, you will likely be ready for first-year college courses.

U.S. Rank and State Rank: Your ranks tell you the approximate percentages of recent high school graduates in the U.S. and your state who took the ACT and received scores that are the same as or lower than yours.

Your Scores: Test scores are not precise measures of educational development. ACT scores reported are the midpoint of a score range that represents your educational development at the time you took the ACT. For example, the score range is plus or minus points for the Composite score. You will find more information interpreting your scores in the *Using Your ACT Results* booklet with this report and at **www.actstudent.org**.

The score ranges from 1 to 36. Writing domain scores range 2 to 12. Domain scores do not necessarily add up to your score the Writing test.

English Language Arts (ELA): An average of your English, Reading, and Writing scores. The score ranges from 1 to 36.

Science, Technology, Engineering, and Mathematics (STEM): An average of your Math and Science scores. The score ranges from 1 to 36.

Understanding Complex Texts: Measures level of proficiency on a subset of items in the Reading test assessing the ability to identify the central meaning and purposes for a range of increasingly complex texts.

Progress Toward Career Readiness: Based on your ACT Composite score, Progress Toward Career Readiness is an indicator of your potential level of achievement on the ACT National Career Readiness Certificate™ (ACT NCRC®). The ACT NCRC is an assessment-based credential that certifies skills critical to your future education and career success.

Learn how ACT NCRC performance relates to job skill requirements at www.act.org/workkeys/briefs/files/NCRCRequirements.pdf.

This information is not to be considered a substitute for actual performance on the ACT NCRC.

Your College Reports

At your direction, your scores from this test date are being reported to the colleges shown below. College planning information is provided for the first four choices you listed when you registered or tested. Check with colleges for recent changes in information. Note: Your GPA was calculated from the grades you reported.

College Name (Code)	Profile of Enrolled 1st-Year Students: ACT Composite Score	High School Class Rank	High School GPA	Preferred Program of Study Availability	Approximate Annual Tuition and Fees: In-state	Out-of-state	Percentage of 1st-Year Students Receiving Financial Aid: Need-based	Merit-based
UNIVERSITY OF OMEGA (9521) OMEGA, CO WWW.UNIVERSITYOFOMEGA.EDU	MIDDLE 50% BETWEEN 18–24	MAJORITY IN TOP 50%	2.76	4-YR DEGREE	$5,600	$12,000	67%	20%
ALPHA UNIVERSITY (9059) UNIVERSITY CENTER, IA WWW.ALPHA.EDU	MIDDLE 50% BETWEEN 21–26	MAJORITY IN TOP 25%	3.12	4-YR DEGREE	$9,000*	$15,000*	85%	27%
BETA COMMUNITY COLLEGE (8866) CLARKSTON, CO WWW.BETACC.EDU	MIDDLE 50% BETWEEN 16–21	MAJORITY IN TOP 75%	2.49	PROGRAM AVAILABLE	$4,000	$4,000	58%	18%
MAGNA COLLEGE (8905) PLAINVIEW, OH WWW.MAGNA.EDU	MIDDLE 50% BETWEEN 21–26	MAJORITY IN TOP 50%	2.71	4-YR DEGREE	$8,500	$14,000	90%	35%

Student Information	Composite Score	Class Rank	Calculated GPA	Selected Major
	21	TOP 25%	3.29	ACCOUNTING

For more information on college and career planning, interpreting your scores, and sending additional score reports, go to www.actstudent.org.

A dash (—) indicates information was not provided or could not be calculated. | *Institution provided cost information that may reflect more than tuition and fees.

www.actstudent.org/scores/understand/studentreport.html

ACT Essay PROMPT – Practice! Practice! Practice!

Intelligent Machines

Many of the goods and services we depend on daily are now supplied by intelligent, automated machines rather than human beings. Robots build cars and other goods on assembly lines, where once there were human workers. Many of our phone conversations are now conducted not with people but with sophisticated technologies. We can now buy goods at a variety of stores without the help of a human cashier. Automation is generally seen as a sign of progress, but what is lost when we replace humans with machines? Given the accelerating variety and prevalence of intelligent machines, it is worth examining the implications and meaning of their presence in our lives.

Read and carefully consider these perspectives. Each suggests a particular way of thinking about the increasing presence of intelligent machines.

Perspective One	Perspective Two	Perspective Three
What we lose with the replacement of people by machines is some part of our own humanity. Even our mundane daily encounters no longer require from us basic courtesy, respect, and tolerance for other people.	Machines are good at low-skill, repetitive jobs, and at high-speed, extremely precise jobs. In both cases they work better than humans. This ef ciency leads to a more prosperous and progressive world for everyone.	Intelligent machines challenge our long-standing ideas about what humans are or can be. This is good because it pushes both humans and machines toward new, unimagined possibilities.

Essay Task

Write a unified, coherent essay in which you evaluate multiple perspectives on the increasing presence of intelligent machines. In your essay, be sure to:

- analyze and evaluate the perspectives given
- state and develop your own perspective on the issue
- explain the relationship between your perspective and those given

Your perspective may be in full agreement with any of the others, in partial agreement, or wholly different. Whatever the case, support your ideas with logical reasoning and detailed, persuasive examples.

www.actstudent.org/writing/sample/

WHEN DO YOU GET YOUR ACT SCORES?

The ACT allows you to register online and view your score report on the Web. For a fee, you can send copies of your score report to multiple institutions.

Students can view their scores through their registered ACT student web accounts. If your scores are not available by the score posting date listed for your particular test date (see next page for examples), make sure to check back on a weekly basis. Scores are processed and updated each week. In normal circumstances, all scores should be reported online within 8 weeks of the test date.

In certain circumstances, scoring can take longer than expected. According to the ACT Corporation, it takes longer to report scores if any of the following hold true:

- The answer documents from your test centre arrived late or your test date was rescheduled.
- You are writing the ACT in Canada, in which case you must allow an additional 1 to 2 weeks for documents to arrive from Canada.
- The Matching Information you provided on the answer sheet (name, date of birth, and Match Number) is not consistent with the Matching Information on your admission ticket.
- An irregularity is reported at your test centre.
- You owe registration fees.
- You tested as a standby.

Sample ACT score release dates (2016-2017)

The following table gives an example of the score posting dates expected for the 2017 examination periods.

National or International Test Dates	Multiple-Choice Scores Posted Online
September 10, 2016	September 20, 2016–November 4, 2016
October 22, 2016	November 8, 2016–December 27, 2016
December 10, 2016	December 20, 2016–February 3, 2017
February 11, 2017	February 22, 2017–April 7, 2017
April 8, 2017	April 18, 2017–June 2, 2017
June 10, 2017	June 20, 2017–August 4, 2017

Visit **http://www.actstudent.org/scores/viewing-scores.html** for updates.

QUICK GUIDE COMPARISON BETWEEN THE SAT AND ACT
STRUCTURE AND FORMAT, SAT VS. ACT

SAT *Four sections, plus an optional essay.*	ACT *Four sections, plus an optional writing section.* *The writing section is usually required by Ivy League Schools.*
Reading **Length:** 65 minutes One 65-minute section **Content:** Reading comprehension **Format:** Multiple choice	**Reading** **Length:** 35 minutes One 35-minute section **Content:** Reading comprehension, vocabulary and word choice, and sentence organization **Format:** Multiple choice
Mathematics **Length:** 80 minutes Two sections totaling 80 minutes **Content**: Number theory, geometry, trigonometry, basic and higher-level algebra, and word problems **Format**: Multiple choice and grid-ins (student-produced responses)	**Mathematics** **Length:** 60 minutes One 60-minute section **Content:** Pre-algebra, algebra I, algebra II, geometry, and trigonometry **Format:** Multiple choice
Writing and Language **Length**: 35 minutes One 35-minute section **Content**: Grammar usage, word choice, organization, and expression of ideas **Format**: Multiple choice	**English** **Length:** 45 minutes One 45-minute section **Content:** Punctuation, grammar and usage, sentence structure and organization **Format:** Multiple choice

SAT	ACT
	Science **Length:** 35 minutes One 35-minute section **Content:** Data representation, research summaries, and conflicting viewpoints **Format:** Multiple choice
Essay (optional) **Length:** 50 minutes **Content:** Analyze the author's usage of evidence, reasoning, and stylistic elements to support their claims	**Writing (optional)** **Length:** 40 minutes **Content:** Analyze and explain the relationship among 3 different perspectives on a given topic while also stating and developing your own perspective. You must also relate your perspective to the other given perspectives.
SAT Top Score: 1600	**ACT Top Score**: 36

Scoring penalty differences, SAT vs. ACT

A key difference to keep in mind when comparing the SAT and the ACT is their respective penalty structures.

The ACT exam does not penalize students for incorrect answers. Therefore, students are encouraged to guess when they do not know the answer.

The old SAT before March 2016 did penalize students for incorrect answers. Special training was required to know when to guess, when to avoid guessing, and how to maximize your scoring potential in each section of the exam. The new SAT does not penalize students for incorrect answers.

Contact PREPSKILLS® for more information about the specialized training courses we run throughout the year!

ADMISSION STATISTICS

SAT/ACT

In the previous section, we provided an example of Princeton University's Admission statistics table. You should always make sure to find out what the SAT or ACT score ranges are for the colleges you are seeking admission to, and then make sure to achieve scores within or above those ranges.

The next few pages have examples of SAT and ACT guidelines, published by various colleges. These guidelines can be found in the admissions section of a college's website. Such guidelines are highly specific to particular institutions. These examples are meant to indicate the variety of ways in which colleges specify their standardized test ranges for applicants.

University of Minnesota

The University of Minnesota acknowledges both SAT and ACT scores, although it does not require the Writing portion for either exam.

From the university's academic and admissions profile page, it is apparent there is no "set" ACT or SAT score. Acceptable scores depend upon the particular program being applied to. If you are applying to liberal arts at Minnesota, your scores can be lower on both exams as compared to the scores required by students applying to the biological sciences. This is because liberal arts admissions staff place greater emphasis on factors other than standardized test scores, in order to determine your quality as a student. They may focus on talents, such as; writing abilities, debating skills, or extra-curricular references, to determine your worthiness as a liberal arts candidate.

Academic Profile

admissions.tc.umn.edu/academics/profile.html

University of Minnesota
Driven to Discover

+ Menu

Academic profile of fall 2015 admitted freshman applicants by college

This table provides a general overview of the middle 50 percentile high school rank and standardized test scores of freshman applicants admitted for fall 2015. Overall, the middle 50 percent of students admitted for fall 2015 scored between a 27 and 31 on the ACT, between an 1830 and 2100 on the SAT, and had a high school rank percentile between 81 and 96.

The data presented in the table are a composite picture of admitted freshman applicants by college; they are not admission criteria. Admission decisions are based on an individual, overall assessment of each application. For complete information on our application review factors, please see our **admissions overview**.

	Biological Sciences	Design	Education & Human Development	Food, Agricultural and Natural Resource Sciences	Liberal Arts	Management (Carlson School of)	Science and Engineering
High School Rank							
High School Rank (if applicable) - Range of the Middle 50 Percentile of Admitted Freshmen	91 - 99%	74 - 92%	80 - 94%	75 - 94%	77 - 93%	87 - 97%	93 - 99%
ACT Composite							
ACT - Range of the Middle 50 Percentile of Admitted Freshmen	29 - 32	25 - 28	23 - 28	25 - 29	26 - 30	28 - 31	30 - 33
SAT Total							
SAT - Range of the Middle 50 Percentile of Admitted Freshmen (SAT total out of 2400)	1890 - 2160	1750 - 1970	1720 - 1940	1740 - 1980	1790 - 2030	1860 - 2060	2000 - 2220

http://admissions.tc.umn.edu/academics/profile.html

IOWA STATE UNIVERSITY

Iowa State consistently ranks as one of the top 50 American colleges. It has a student body numbering more than 26,000 students. To weed through the thousands of applications it receives every year, the university has developed its own admissions standards algorithm known as the **Regent Admission Index.**

This index is calculated based upon ACT scores. If you choose to take the SAT instead, your SAT scores will be converted into an ACT equivalency. It is to your advantage, to take the ACT rather than the SAT for this particular college. **If you achieve a 245 overall RAI score, you gain automatic entry to Iowa State.**

Regent Admission Index

Students who wish to enter Iowa State University directly from high school will be admitted based upon their Regent Admission Index (RAI) score. There are two mathematical formulas for computing student's RAI scores, the primary RAI formula (for students whose high school provides class rank) and the Alternative RAI formula (for students whose high school does not provide class rank). Below is a detailed description of each formula:

Primary RAI Formula (for students whose high school provides class rank)	Alternative RAI Formula (for students whose high school does NOT provide class rank)
Percentile class rank x 1 + ACT composite score x 2 + Cumulative GPA x 20 + Number of years of high school core courses x 5 RAI score	ACT composite score x 3 + Cumulative GPA x 30 + Number of years of high school core courses x 5 RAI score

Note: For purposes of calculating the RAI, SAT scores will be converted to ACT composite equivalents; high school rank is expressed as a percentile with 99% as the top value; high school GPA is expressed on a 4-point scale; and number of high school courses completed in the core subject areas is expressed in terms of years or fractions of years of study.

Applicants who achieve at least a 245 RAI score and who meet the minimum high school course requirements will automatically be offered admission. Applicants who achieve less than a 245 RAI score and who meet the minimum high school course requirements may also be offered admission, but their applications will be reviewed on an individual basis.

http://www.admissions.iastate.edu/freshman/requirements.php?action=entry

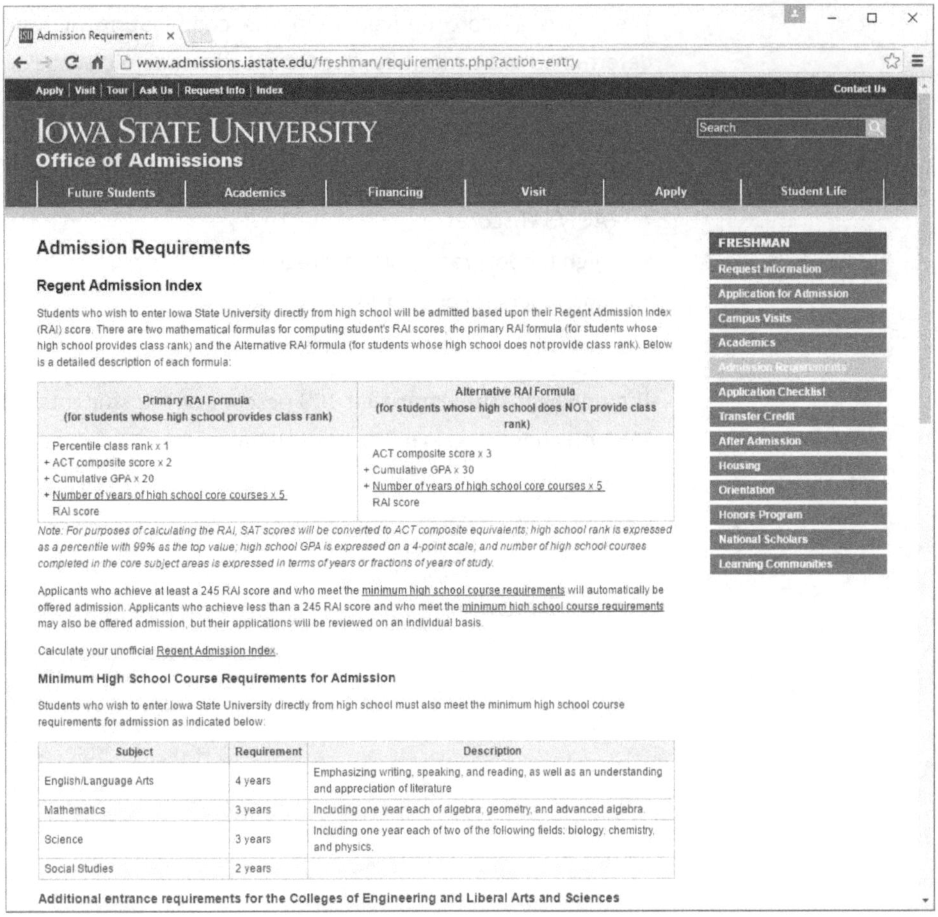

Admission Requirements

www.admissions.iastate.edu/freshman/requirements.php?action=entry

Apply | Visit | Tour | Ask Us | Request Info | Index — Contact Us

IOWA STATE UNIVERSITY
Office of Admissions

Future Students | Academics | Financing | Visit | Apply | Student Life

Admission Requirements

Regent Admission Index

Students who wish to enter Iowa State University directly from high school will be admitted based upon their Regent Admission Index (RAI) score. There are two mathematical formulas for computing student's RAI scores, the primary RAI formula (for students whose high school provides class rank) and the Alternative RAI formula (for students whose high school does not provide class rank). Below is a detailed description of each formula:

Primary RAI Formula (for students whose high school provides class rank)	Alternative RAI Formula (for students whose high school does NOT provide class rank)
Percentile class rank x 1 + ACT composite score x 2 + Cumulative GPA x 20 + Number of years of high school core courses x 5 RAI score	ACT composite score x 3 + Cumulative GPA x 30 + Number of years of high school core courses x 5 RAI score

Note: For purposes of calculating the RAI, SAT scores will be converted to ACT composite equivalents; high school rank is expressed as a percentile with 99% as the top value; high school GPA is expressed on a 4-point scale; and number of high school courses completed in the core subject areas is expressed in terms of years or fractions of years of study.

Applicants who achieve at least a 245 RAI score and who meet the minimum high school course requirements will automatically be offered admission. Applicants who achieve less than a 245 RAI score and who meet the minimum high school course requirements may also be offered admission, but their applications will be reviewed on an individual basis.

Calculate your unofficial Regent Admission Index.

Minimum High School Course Requirements for Admission

Students who wish to enter Iowa State University directly from high school must also meet the minimum high school course requirements for admission as indicated below:

Subject	Requirement	Description
English/Language Arts	4 years	Emphasizing writing, speaking, and reading, as well as an understanding and appreciation of literature
Mathematics	3 years	Including one year each of algebra, geometry, and advanced algebra.
Science	3 years	Including one year each of two of the following fields: biology, chemistry, and physics.
Social Studies	2 years	

Additional entrance requirements for the Colleges of Engineering and Liberal Arts and Sciences

FRESHMAN
Request Information
Application for Admission
Campus Visits
Academics
Admission Requirements
Application Checklist
Transfer Credit
After Admission
Housing
Orientation
Honors Program
National Scholars
Learning Communities

WHY DOES IOWA STATE USE THE RAI?

In the spring of 2006, the Iowa State legislature passed a piece of legislation known as the House File 2395. That law required the Board of Regents, at the state's college, to conduct a study of the "upper-half class rank requirement"— the tool Iowa State University had used since 1958, to accept or decline applications. The Board found the requirement favoured top scorers on standardized tests, as well as students with high GPAs.

An Admissions Study Team was created to research the issue, and after completing its review of the past five decades of Iowa State acceptance standards, the Team created the **Regent Admission Index (RAI)**, recommending that the RAI replace the current upper-half class rank requirement. The Iowa State legislature approved the new set of standards and it went into effect for freshmen who entered Iowa State-funded universities beginning in the fall of 2009.

The RAI is a score derived from the combination of **four factors**, which the Team determined were the best predictors of academic success. Those factors include the following:

- high school class rank
- ACT/SAT scores
- high school grade point average
- core courses completed

The university stipulates that 100 percent of the students whose combined RAI score is 245 or higher will gain entry into the university.

University of California—Los Angeles (UCLA)

The University of California—Los Angeles (UCLA) accepts both the SAT and the ACT composite exams. It also specifies that certain SAT Subject Tests are required for general admission.

Below is a copy of the student profile and SAT and ACT score ranges for UCLA applicants, for the 2015 academic year.

http://www.admission.ucla.edu/prospect/adm_fr/Frosh_Prof15.htm

Profile of Admitted Fresh

www.admissions.ucla.edu/prospect/adm_fr/Frosh_Prof15.htm

UCLA Undergraduate Admission

Search Admissions with Google

PROSPECTIVE STUDENTS | CURRENT APPLICANTS | ADMITTED STUDENTS | TOURS | CONTACT

PROFILE OF ADMITTED FRESHMEN FALL 2015

When we review our freshman applicants, we look at a wide variety of factors, some more easily quantifiable than others. Below are the primary academic factors we considered when we reviewed our freshman applicants for Fall Quarter 2015. There is no specific cutoff value assigned to any of the factors we consider.

Overview by Residency

	California Residents	Out-of-State	International	Total
Applicants	57,756	18,645	16,327	**92,728**
Admits	9,358	4,323	2,335	**16,016**
Enrolled	4,083	954	643	5,680
Admit Rate	16%	23%	14%	17%
Enroll Rate	44%	22%	28%	35%
% of Total Applicants	62%	20%	18%	100%

ACADEMIC STATISTICS

Notes:

- All **GPAs** are calculated from courses taken in grades 10 and 11.
  - The **Fully Weighted GPA** includes an extra grade point for all UC-approved honors courses (which include AP, IB, school-based honors, and transferable college courses) in which a grade of C or higher is earned. The maximum value possible is 5.00.
  - This **Unweighted GPA** does not include any extra grade points for honors courses. The maximum value possible is 4.00.
- **Honors Courses** included in the totals below are taken in grades 10–12, and are counted by semester, which means a year-long high school honors course would count as two. A single-semester course would count as one.
- **Domestic** refers to applicants who are US citizens, permanent residents, refugees, or asylees.

Averages and Quartiles – Applicants

	Average	25th Percentile	75th Percentile
Fully Weighted GPA	3.95	3.68	4.30
Unweighted GPA	3.59	3.38	3.90
ACT Composite	28	25	32
SAT Composite	1844	1640	2070

AMERICAN COLLEGE LISTINGS

US ★ COLLEGE EXPO™ CANADA
VANCOUVER ★ CALGARY ★ OTTAWA ★ TORONT

There are many "degree navigator" and "college navigator" websites online today. You may want to consult a few of them to get a sense of which universities best cater to your professional and academic goals.

If you are looking for a listing of all the colleges (both public and private) by state, or alphabetically, the sites listed in the box to the right will be of use to you.

Many high schools in Canada also host university fairs, where it is possible to find American colleges advertising their undergraduate programs. Ask your school counsellor whether a university or college fair is in town and how you can register to attend it.

Visit www.USCollegeExpo.com and register to attend the next U.S. College Expo in Canada! It's your best opportunity to meet with U.S. college representatives in Canada!

Speaking with university representatives directly is an excellent means of determining whether a particular university is what you're looking for or whether you've been misled by reputation and hype.

Online college listings

One of the first places to look for a searchable listing of American colleges is: ***collegeboard.org***

Collegeboard.org also hosts a college-matching system, which can help you locate colleges and departments that cater to your academic or sports needs: https://bigfuture.collegeboard.org/majors-careers

Compiled by the University of Texas at Austin, this site lists colleges by state: *www.utexas.edu/world/univ/state*

Compiled by a consortium of organizations, known collectively as Colleges.com, this navigating tool is useful in locating colleges by searching for the particular program of interest to you: *www.colleges.com/admissions/collegesearch/index.html*

COLLEGE NAVIGATOR SITES

There are a number of websites that offer students an easy means of comparing colleges (see the list on the previous page). One of the most comprehensive and trustworthy **college navigator** websites is run by the **U.S. Department of Education**. It allows students to search colleges and universities by location, type (public, private, etc.), degree program, awards, scholarships, and name.

http://nces.ed.gov/collegenavigator/

Another highly useful website is the college search site run by the **College Board**. This site allows students to compare colleges and universities according to location, cost, program of study, and student profiles.

https://bigfuture.collegeboard.org/college-search

PICKING AND CHOOSING

Although an infinite number of considerations might come into play when you start considering colleges, there are a few key considerations you should take into account as you whittle down your list of potential options.

In making the following considerations, you are likely to find a more suitable match for your career goals, personality, academic or athletic pursuits.

SIZE OF THE STUDENT BODY

Big universities are not always the best idea; the larger the student body, the more demand there is for basic services, including; individual time with tutors and professors, availability of books in the library, openings for campus jobs, and access to medical services. A small university will generally boast fewer than 2,000 students on campus; a mid-range university will contain anywhere from 2,000 to 15,000 students; a large university will usually host more than 15,000 students.

If your focus is on academic success, you should seriously consider the size of the student body, not only at the college in general but also within your specific program of interest. For example, if you are planning to go into engineering, find out how many students there are in a general, first-year, mathematics or engineering course. At big universities, there can be over 1,000 students, in a huge lecture hall, with you. At smaller universities, the number might only be 100. In the latter instance, you will certainly find you will have more personal access to your professors and tutors/teaching assistants.

LOCATION

If you want your university experience to be as much about life learning as it is about in-class learning, consider the location of the school. Many well-known schools are located in small towns. For example, Princeton University is located in Princeton, New Jersey. It is half way between New York and Philadelphia, but it is not in either cities. If you prefer small-town life, then it might be a good choice for you. If you're hoping for urban living, with all of the varied experiences of big city life, then Princeton might not be a great choice for you.

By contrast, New York University—one of the largest private universities in the U.S.A—is located in the heart of New York, with campus offices and buildings strewn across Manhattan. Depending on your program choice, living in a big city can be a boon to your university career. It means, in addition to the university facilities, you can access city and state libraries, and other major attractions, such as; museums, galleries, and major political institutions.

Your program choice, and your individual personality, should determine which sort of location you desire for your university experience.

RANGE OF ACADEMIC PROGRAMS

Large universities, such as NYU and Princeton, will offer a multitude of program choices—everything from sociology and anthropology, to medieval languages and civil engineering.

Smaller universities, such as the Albany College of Pharmacy and Health Sciences, will offer fewer programs overall, as they focus on particular course programs. Small universities pay specific attention to the reputation and resources allocated to their flagship programs. At Albany College, the focus is on pharmacy and health sciences, hence the name.

Some small and mid-sized universities also specialise in group-oriented social dynamics. For instance, there are a number of women-only and men-only colleges that cater to those people who prefer mono-gendered learning environments. Other colleges, such as the American Indian colleges, specialise in welcoming people from First Nations and Aboriginal communities. There are also a number of African-American universities specializing in welcoming people from visible minority communities. There are also religious-based colleges, which cater to practitioners of various faiths.

Community specific colleges

Aboriginal colleges

In an effort to draw in more students from disadvantaged socio-economic backgrounds, a number of aboriginal (First Nations or "American Indian") colleges have opened up over the years, proving to be a resounding success.

Many of these colleges offer demographic-specific scholarships and bursaries; they also offer cultural and linguistic programming, which aim to revivify or maintain endangered aboriginal languages across the U.S.A. One such institution is Haskell Indian Nations University (Lawrence, Kansas) which enrols over 1,000 students per semester. For information on these schools, and funding opportunities, consult the following website:

American Indian College Fund
www.collegefund.org/about/main.html

African-American colleges

There are over 100 African-American colleges in the United States and they are often grouped under the overarching heading "Historically black colleges and universities" (HBCUs). These institutions are a mix of public and private institutions; some are religiously-oriented as well.

HBCUs are *not* exclusively African-American, even though their student populations predominantly hail from visible minority communities. Some examples include Alabama State University (Montgomery, Alabama), Savannah State University (Savannah, Georgia) and Kentucky State University (Frankfort, Kentucky).

United Negro College Fund
www.uncf.org

Women's colleges

There are dozens of women's colleges across the United States. The vast majority are private institutions, although there are some publicly-funded schools as well, including; Rutgers University (New Brunswick, New Jersey), Texas Women's University (Denton, Texas), and Mississippi University for Women (Columbus, Mississippi).

For more information about the history of women's colleges and the diversity of such institutions, consult the following website:

www.womenscolleges.org

Religious colleges

There are a plethora of religiously focused private universities in the United States. Many of these schools are considered small colleges. Some have student populations that number fewer than 100 students. The vast majority of religious schools in the U.S. are Christian-based. The Council for Christian Colleges and Universities might be a useful starting point for those interested in this type of university setting.

Council for Christian Colleges and Universities
www.cccu.org

There are also a number of Jewish colleges in the U.S. A well-known example is the American Jewish University located in Bel Air, California. There is one accredited Hindu university in the U.S., it is Hindu University of America (also known as the International Vedic Hindu University) located in Orlando, Florida. There are a handful of accredited Buddhist universities in the U.S., the best known of which is Naropa University in Boulder, Colorado. Currently, there are no accredited Muslim- or Sikh-based universities or colleges in the U.S.

For more information on faith-based schooling, students are advised to search online for specific universities, as there is no over-arching organization that disseminates information on religious schooling.

Student Life on Campus

Oftentimes, you will find yourself sick of studying in your room or at the library. Being able to choose from a variety of socially active places to go, and work, is a useful additive to any campus experience. The best way to determine whether a particular university has the sort of campus life you're seeking is to visit the campus, at some point, before you apply.

A safe, comfortable, and socially-inviting campus life is the key to success for many students. The sorts of student life services you ought to consider in your campus tour, include; the availability of bars, pubs, cafes, lounges, and 24-hour computer labs and study spaces.

Cost

Many state-level universities are "public", in the sense that a large portion of their operational funding is provided by an annual grant from the state (i.e. the University of Florida is funded by the State of Florida; the University of California is funded by the State of California, and so on).

These colleges work on a funding system that is more comparable to the Canadian system, in that government pays for part of the student's tuition and the student pays for the rest, in the form of tuition fees.

As of the 2015-2016 academic year, the average cost of educating a typical undergraduate student in the United States without room and board ranges from approximately $9,000 to $33,000. At public colleges, students pay tuition fees that range (depending on program of study, state location, the size of classes, etc.) between $9,000/year and $24,000/year. The deficit is filled by money from the state. It is for this reason that state colleges and public colleges are less expensive institutions to study at.

At fully private institutions, which include all the Ivy Leagues schools (except Cornell, which does get some public money for operational costs associated with certain departments), the student must bear the full cost of his or her tuition. That means, tuition rates at private institutions are usually higher than those at public institutions. As of the 2015-2016 academic year, the average tuition rate at private, non-profit institutions rose to $32,405/year.

You might wonder why some colleges choose to be private rather than public. The reasons are complex and they are largely political and historical in nature. Because public institutions receive public funds, they are accountable to (democratically-elected) state governments (i.e. the taxpayer). State governments retain the theoretical ability to determine how public money is spent at the universities they fund. Private institutions, are not tied to government sources. In theory, they are free to teach what they want in any manner they wish, and spend their money as they see fit.

Average undergraduate tuition and fees, and room and board rates charged for full-time students in degree-granting institutions, by type and control of institution

Constant 2012–13 dollars
Total tuition, room and board

All institutions			
	All institutions	4-year	2-year
1982–83	$9,138	$10,385	$6,396
1992–93	$12,097	$14,216	$6,830
2001–02	$14,775	$17,708	$7,424
2002–03	$15,262	$18,344	$7,943
2003–04	$16,104	$19,276	$8,336
2004–05	$16,647	$19,925	$8,563
2005–06	$17,014	$20,289	$8,412
2006–07	$17,547	$20,934	$8,461
2007–08	$17,737	$21,160	$8,346
2008–09	$18,421	$21,996	$8,879
2009–10	$18,839	$22,515	$9,109
2010–11	$19,355	$23,118	$9,323
2011–12	$19,741	$23,409	$9,461
2012–13	$20,234	$23,872	$9,574

Public institutions			
	All institutions	4-year	2-year
1982–83	$6,941	$7,534	$5,632
1992–93	$8,731	$9,772	$6,166
2001–02	$10,415	$11,940	$6,670
2002–03	$10,800	$12,434	$7,116
2003–04	$11,496	$13,270	$7,474
2004–05	$11,905	$13,790	$7,694
2005–06	$12,154	$14,077	$7,547
2006–07	$12,522	$14,503	$7,723
2007–08	$12,647	$14,675	$7,623
2008–09	$13,209	$15,371	$8,156
2009–10	$13,667	$16,027	$8,223
2010–11	$14,194	$16,657	$8,460
2011–12	$14,616	$17,084	$8,715
2012–13	$15,022	$17,474	$8,928

Private nonprofit and for-profit institutions			
	All institutions	4-year	2-year
1982–83	$16,311	$16,797	$12,644
1992–93	$23,754	$24,364	$16,076
2001–02	$29,100	$29,727	$20,547
2002–03	$29,652	$30,220	$22,554
2003–04	$30,613	$31,167	$24,315
2004–05	$31,158	$31,693	$24,497
2005–06	$31,284	$31,778	$24,885
2006–07	$32,231	$32,774	$22,988
2007–08	$32,530	$33,032	$23,698
2008–09	$33,199	$33,706	$24,494
2009–10	$33,116	$33,612	$26,134
2010–11	$33,513	$34,131	$24,979
2011–12	$33,608	$34,234	$24,049
2012–13	$34,483	$35,074	$23,328

Constant dollars based on the Consumer Price Index, prepared by the Bureau of Labor Statistics, U.S. Department of Labor, adjusted to a school-year basis.
'SOURCE: U.S. Department of Education, National Center for Education Statistics (2015). Digest of Education Statistics, 2013 (NCES 2015-011),Table 330.10.. (This table was prepared Jan 2016.)

Those theoretical pictures are not, however, entirely accurate descriptions of actual practice.

In reality, most state-funded (i.e. public) colleges possess highly independent, internal governing structures; they are also protected from direct governmental interference by state-level educational legislation.

Meanwhile, private colleges are not actually free to teach whatever they want, in any manner they wish. For an institution to have its degrees accredited and recognized as legitimate, it must subscribe to certain educational standards and curricular demands, which have been standardized for the purposes of ensuring that degrees are comparable, in quality, across the country (i.e. transferable in terms of the skills set that graduates possess).

It is for this reason that a chemistry degree from the University of Florida is comparable to a chemistry degree from the University of Alaska, which is comparable to a chemistry degree from Harvard University.

To get a better sense of the range in tuition costs across the United States, consider the table of tuition rates provided on the previous pages. Remember that private tuition rates do not reflect superior quality teaching. Rather, they reflect an alternative funding structure—one of which is based upon independent financial management by the college.

National Centre for Education Statistics

Comparing tuition rates

The tables on the previous page demonstrate the tuition differences between public and private colleges in the United States.

Note that in the 2015-2016 academic year, the average tuition rate for four-year programs at non-state public colleges was $9,410/year. By contrast, the average tuition for four-year programs at private, non-profit colleges was $32,405/year.*

**Tuition means all academic tuition costs and any additional fees, such as student registration and campus and health service fees.*

RESOURCES FOR DETERMINING WHICH COLLEGE IS BEST FOR YOU

Ultimately, in deciding which college(s) to apply to, students need to consider their academic and professional goals, as well as their individual personalities and their expectations of the "college experience."

Since it's not feasible to visit every campus you might want to attend, it's helpful to consider detailed accounts of college life, which, scholars, journalists, and educationalists, have produced in order to help you make this decision. The references provided in the box to the right include examples of such accounts.

Choosing your college

The Fiske Guide to Colleges, by Edward B. Fiske and Robert Logue.

The Insider's Guide to the Colleges, by Yale Daily News.

Looking Beyond the Ivy League: Finding the College That's Right for You, by Loren Pope.

Colleges that Change Lives, by Loren Pope.

RANKINGS

Various organizations offer college rankings. Beware - there are differing **statistical methodologies** used to generate particular ranking tables.

Some of the factors considered in generating a ranking list include (but are not limited to) the following: size of classes; ranges of degree options; specificity of degree options; opportunities for internships in particular programs; scholarship and bursary availability; availability of technical degrees (such as law, medicine, and business administration); financial success of alumni; and student, alumni, and professorial surveys.

You will find a number of ranking systems listed on the following pages. Each system uses a different series of factors to distinguish between top-performing colleges. Consequently, each system produces different results for its top colleges.

NATIONAL AMERICAN RANKINGS

U.S. News Best Colleges Rankings (annual ranking) ranks national universities, liberal arts colleges, business programs, and engineering programs. In September 2015, U.S. News & World Report ranked Princeton University as the number one university nation-wide for 2016.

http://colleges.usnews.rankingsandreviews.com/college

The Washington Monthly's College Rankings produced its first (and very controversial), comprehensive report in 2005 (published in 2006) entitled "Is our students learning?" That report offered American university, and college, rankings based upon how well the college had performed as an engine for social mobility (i.e. the survey researched whether colleges helped the poor to get rich and educated or whether they helped the rich to get even richer and more educated). Washington Monthly's ranking considered the degree to which colleges fostered scientific and humanistic research, and the degree to which they promoted an ethic of public service. That report ranked the Massachusetts Institute of Technology (MIT) as its number one university in 2005. The more recent 2009 ranking lists MIT at number 12. The new top national university for 2015 was the University of California – San Diego. Meanwhile, the Washington Monthly's top liberal arts college in 2015 was Bryn Mawr College.

http://www.washingtonmonthly.com/college_guide/rankings-2015/national-universities-rank.php

Forbes magazine online, Forbes.com, published a list of "America's Best Colleges" in 2008. In association with the Centre for College Affordability and Productivity, the Forbes ranking used an Alumni Who's Who in America, student evaluations at www.ratemyprofessors.com, four-year graduation rates, enrolment-adjusted numbers of students and faculty who had received nationally competitive awards, and four-year accumulated student debt, in order to calculate its ranking list. That ranking further separated colleges into top overall, public and private schools.

The college that topped Forbes's "overall" listing in 2015 was Pomona College.

http://www.forbes.com/top-colleges/list/

INTERNATIONAL RANKINGS

The Times Higher Education, a British publication that reports on higher education news, in association with Quacquarelli Symonds, publishes the THES - QS World University Rankings—a listing of 500 universities from around the world. The list included many non-American universities (especially British schools) in its upper tier of top colleges and universities. The THES - QS ranking uses a "peer review" system, which incorporates the views of more than 3000 scholars and academics working in various research fields. For the 2015-2016 academic year, the Times Higher Education, in partnership with Elsevier, ranked California Institute of Technology as its top university worldwide in its World University Rankings.

https://www.timeshighereducation.com/world-university-rankings/2016/world-ranking#!/page/0/length/25

MONEY MATTERS

Without money, you simply can't go to school. If you happen to hail from a wealthy background, then money might not be a concern for you. But for the vast majority of students, money matters.

Whether you come from a well-off family, or you fund your studies and living expenses entirely on your own, budgeting for the future is an important skill to develop early on.

Knowing where to find funding—e.g. scholarships, bursaries, and student loans—is a crucial skill to possess. This section will help you develop that skill, by describing resources related to scholarships and student loans.

SCHOLARSHIPS: MERIT-BASED, NEED-BASED, AND SPECIALITY SCHOLARSHIPS

Merit-based scholarships go to students who are superior academic performers. They are usually awarded on a competitive basis. A key example includes the National Merit Scholarships (based on PSAT scores).

Need-based scholarships go to students whose financial resources restrict them from attending a college or university to which they have been accepted. Such scholarships are available at many schools and they can be quite large, depending on the financial-aid resources at the college in question.

Specialty scholarships include specific funds that many colleges set aside for awards based on particular identifications, ethnic backgrounds, religious affiliations, or other talents and skills. Often, the funds are provided by alumni associations or other private benefactors. Some examples, include; scholarships for students from certain religious denominations, particular geographic areas, or for students with unique disabilities.

If you know you have high grades, then you should be applying for **merit scholarships**. Oftentimes, application deadlines for university scholarships are as early as one year before you enter university. Be prepared to start applying by the end of Grade 11.

If your grades have been a mixed bag of highs and lows, you should still apply for academic scholarships. The majority of scholarships take into consideration, more than grades alone. Oftentimes, scholarship applications will emphasize extra-curricular activities, such as; involvement in student organizations, community volunteering, sports clubs, and part-time employment, in determining who qualifies for scholarship money.

Scholarship manuals and compendia

Scholarships, Grants and Prizes. Published annually by Peterson's (Lawrenceville, NJ).This guide can be ordered at: https://www.petersons.com/college-search/college-scholarships-grants-book.aspx

The Ultimate Scholarship Book: Billions of Dollars in Scholarships, Grants and Prizes, by Gen and Kelly Tanabe. Published annually by SuperCollege, LLC (Belmont, CA), this can be ordered at: http://www.ultimatescholarshipbook.com/

Getting Financial Aid, by The College Board (New York, NY). This guide can be ordered at https://store.collegeboard.org/sto/enter.do

Official Athletic College Guide Baseball, by Charlie Kadupski (Editor). Published by The Sport Source, it can be ordered from Amazon.

As a Canadian student applying to American universities, you are limited in terms of the kinds of scholarships you can apply for. Many scholarships, such as the National Merit Scholarship, are for American students only. Meanwhile, many Canadian government scholarships are for Canadian universities only. Before you apply for any particular scholarship, make sure to read the fine print of the scholarship qualification instructions. There is no point in spending days completing an application for an award you are disqualified from winning because you do not fit the criteria.

Places to look for scholarships

School counsellors—high school counsellors often have the most up-to-date information regarding scholarships available at your high school (i.e. graduation awards). They also have information on scholarships provided by your local school board as well as the federal, provincial, and local governments.

Community organizations—some, long-standing, community organizations have ongoing, long-term scholarship funds. Bodies such as The Knights of Columbus, The Rotary Club, Kiwanis International, Boy Scouts and Girl Scouts, The Lions Club, and Optimist International fund annual scholarships of various amounts.

Parent's employer—if your parent works for a long-standing business in the community, or a branch of government/public services (such as the police force, the fire-fighting force, the local municipality, or town council), chances are there is money available for you through their company or employer scholarship fund.

Unions—if your parents (or you!) are members of a workplace union, find out whether there is an educational fund available through that organization.

Internet scholarship search engines

Some of the following sites are specific to American colleges, while others advertise scholarships and grants in general.

- SuperCollege
  www.supercollege.com
- SallieMae
  https://www.salliemae.com/plan-for-college/
- BrokeScholar
  www.brokescholar.com
- College Xpress
  www.collegexpress.com
- The College Board
  www.collegeboard.org
- Scholarships.com
  www.scholarships.com
- Adventures in Education
  www.aie.org
- CollegeNET
  www.collegenet.com

Military service—if your parents, or grandparents, have served with the Canadian military, there is a good chance some funding for post-secondary schooling might be available for you.

The Internet—over the years, a number of scholarship-based websites have cropped up online. It is worthwhile spending some time on those sites. Register to receive updates on new scholarships posted online.

Scholarship manuals and guidebooks—a number of comprehensive scholarship manuals exist, many of which can be of use to Canadian students. Comprehensive scholarship and grant guidebooks can be helpful in highlighting specific awards you might qualify for. These manuals include listings of all awards available at American colleges, especially those based on professional career goals, academic background, sports affiliations, and community involvement. Students can also search for awards based on ethnicity, membership in visible minority communities, and gender.

College-based scholarships—as with Canadian universities, many colleges in the United States have a scholarship fund that is doled out based on particular merit- or need-based criteria. Sometimes you do not have to apply separately for college scholarships—your entrance application serves as an automatic scholarship application. For example, once you have been accepted by the college, you will be informed as to whether you have been awarded an entrance scholarship of some sort.

Sometimes, your entrance application does not serve as an automatic scholarship application. Make sure to visit the awards page on the colleges website you intend to apply to, in order to determine whether this is the case. Note that every college will differ in this respect. Sometimes the awards and scholarship division of the university is located within the finance department. Sometimes it is a department on its own. In both cases, the college will possess a list of all the scholarships it offers and it will describe the application procedure required to apply for the award(s) in question.

SCHOLARSHIP CASE STUDY

UNIVERSITY OF FLORIDA

The University of Florida's Admissions website contains a link that offers you detailed scholarship information:

http://www.admissions.ufl.edu/scholarships.html

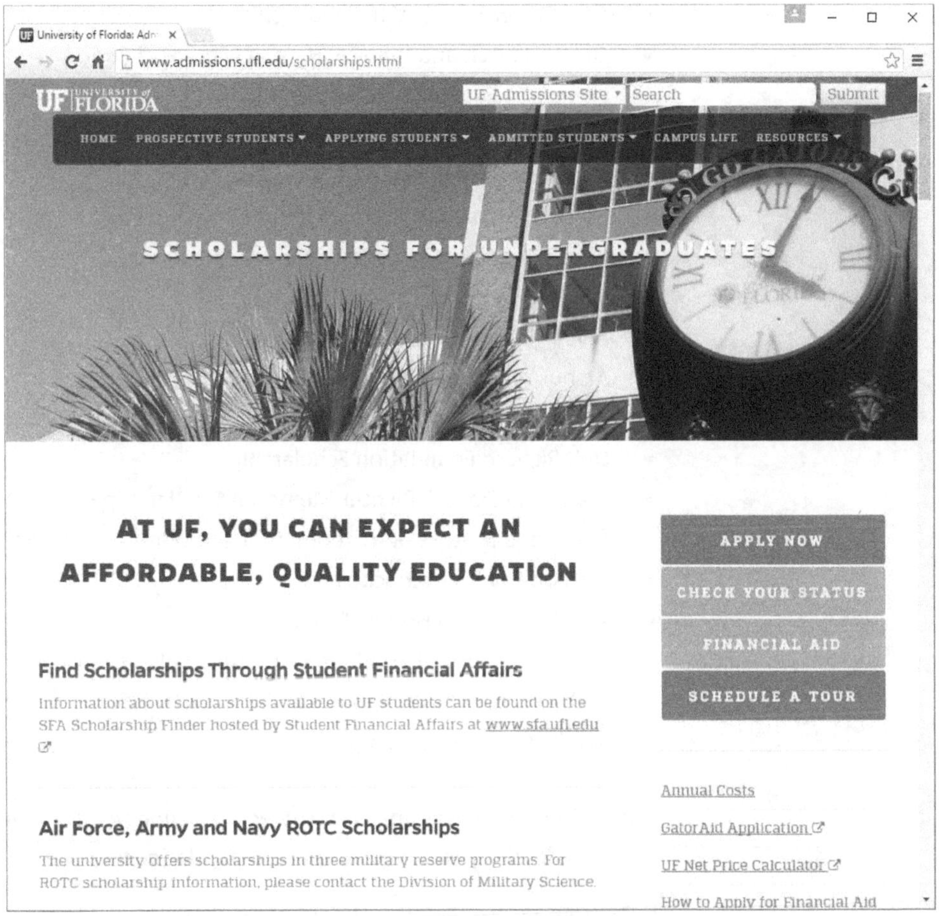

You will find that the university offers varied entrance scholarships administered through its admissions bureau. Some of its endowed scholarships include:

- Alfred T. Airth General Scholarship Fund
- Alumni Graduate Fellowships Fund
- Jerome Bain Scholarship Fund
- Col. Walter E. Barker Merit Scholarship
- Haydon Burns Scholarship Fund
- Thomas C. Chubb Merit Scholarship Fund
- Daniel Leroy Claville, Jr., Scholarship Fund
- Gulf Power Foundation Scholarship
- Grace Hausch and John M. Hausch Memorial Fund
- Irving and ElnaKallman Scholarship Fund
- L. Gale Lemerand Scholarship Fund
- Roger Long/W. J. and A. C. Wise Scholarship Fund
- Bernard F. Masseria Scholarship/Fellowship Fund
- Alfred A. McKethan Scholarship
- Wilma D. Meyer Scholarship Fund
- AlyceNorine Haines Fellowship Fund
- Arthur W. Pugsley Memorial Fund
- Albert G. Raybun Scholarship Fund
- Deb Richard Foundation Scholarship
- Frank and Doris S. Richter Memorial Scholarship Fund
- Sherwood L. Stokes-Environmental and Water Quality Scholarships
- Richard Fay Warner Scholarship Fund
- A. F. Wentworth Honors Scholarship
- Sara H. Woodruff Foundation Graduate Fellowships
- Ted Wysocki Scholarship Fund
- Sue K. Young Scholarship

Note: These scholarships are subject to change every year, so please check the university's admissions web pages on a regular basis.

Most colleges are like the University of Florida, in that they offer a series of privately endowed scholarships. Applications for these scholarships is sometimes automatic—you are automatically considered for each award based on your application for entry to the college in question. In other cases, application is not automatic.

The college's admission's office will be able to tell you which scholarships must be applied for separately. **Remember: deadlines for some scholarship applications may come before you know whether you've been accepted to the college!**

MONEY FOR CANADIANS

As a Canadian, you're probably interested in scholarships and other forms of funding available to Canadians who aim to study in the U.S. The following is an annotated list of funding sources you should consider in your financial planning.

AMMSA: Scholarships for Aboriginal Students
AMMSA publishes a guide to scholarships and bursaries for aboriginal students. The guide currently lists more than 375 scholarships and bursaries.

http://www.ammsa.com/community-access/scholarships/

TD Canada Trust Scholarships
The TD Canada Trust Scholarships for Community Leadership provide up to $10,000 per year for tuition and $7,500 per year for living expenses for up to four years (total of $70,000).

https://www.tdcanadatrust.com/products-services/banking/student-life/scholarship-for-community-leadership/index.jsp

The U.S. colleges themselves
Many U.S. colleges offer scholarships and financial services to Canadian students. For example, Liberty University offers scholarships, such as the Liberty Champion Scholarship and the Early Deposit Award, for residential Canadian applicants. Therefore, it's best to contact admissions offices and browse the financial aid web pages of the universities' websites.

http://www.liberty.edu/undergrad/?PID=22601

Student Loans

Students from Canada can also apply for Canadian federal and provincial student loans. However, the Canadian government will want to know why you've chosen to study outside of Canada.

If you win an academic, or athletic scholarship, to an American college, or you have sufficient reason for wanting to study abroad, you can apply for student loans to help offset your living costs and any remaining tuition costs.

If you have no reason, other than simply wanting to live abroad, your student loan application may not be successful.

The Canadian government values Canadian educational institutions, and given that Canada offers some of the highest quality post-secondary education in the world, the case for wanting to study abroad using taxpayer-funded student loans becomes a difficult one to make.

In preparing your student loan application, be prepared to argue the case for why you need to study abroad. In so doing, consider the following questions: Is there a special program available at your American college that has no equivalent in Canada? Do you have family living in the U.S. that could support you? Do you have a partial scholarship that will help to offset the costs of studying outside of Canada? Are you hoping to study in a specialist degree program, such as the fine arts, theatre, or music, for which particular schools in the U.S. offer a better chance of employment afterward?

If you can answer a definite yes to any of the questions above, your chances of getting a student loan will be improved significantly.

FEDERAL CANADIAN STUDENT LOANS

The Canada Student Loan program is run by the federal government's Human Resources and Skills Development Canada office. You can find their website at the following web address:

http://www.esdc.gc.ca/en/student_loans/government.page

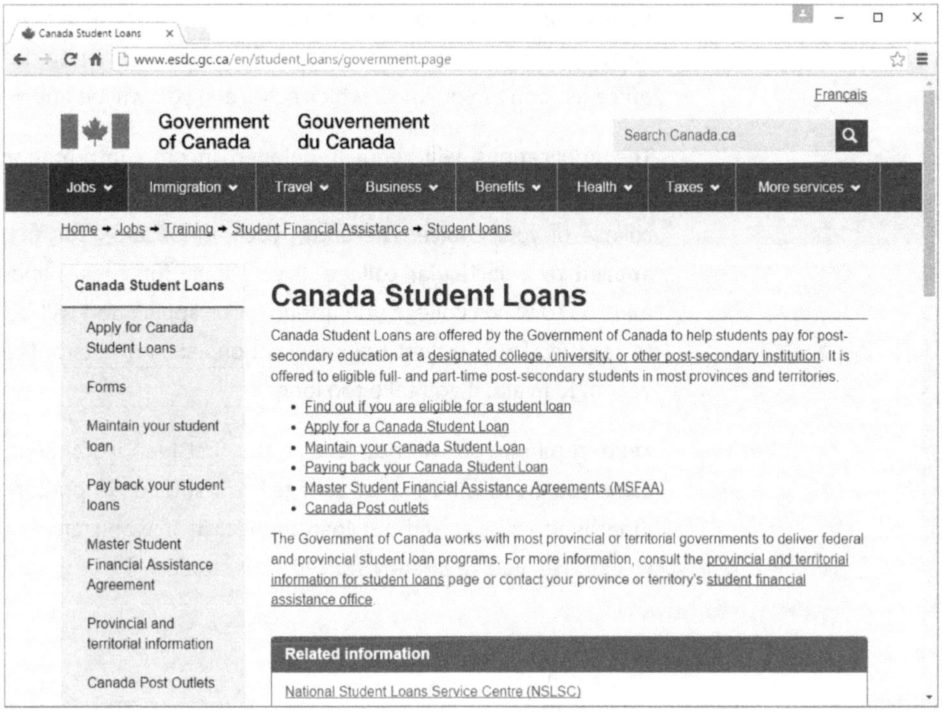

The Canadian government only grants loans to students who choose to study at designated institutions. Before making your application, it is best to confirm your college or university actually appears on that designation list, which can be found at:

http://www.esdc.gc.ca/en/post_secondary/designated_schools.page

To locate your college or university, click on the link for **International institutions**.

Provincial Student Loans

As a Canadian student planning to study abroad, you can (and should) apply for a student loan through your respective provincial government. In general, students studying abroad will receive a joint federal-provincial student loan (as most provincial student loans are focused on helping students attend provincial universities). Nevertheless, there is provincial money available for study at international schools.

Given that provincial student loan programs are constantly being revised and updated so as to reflect the most recent federal and provincial budgetary constraints, you should locate your province's student loan office from the list on the next page and contact the office as soon as you know which college(s) you will be applying to.

The applications will request detailed income information from yourself and your guardians/parents. They also require you to enter specific tuition information for the college of your choice. Therefore, you cannot apply for a student loan **until you have applied to a particular college.** If you apply for a loan, and subsequently change your mind as to which college you attend, your application will be nullified and you will have to reapply. Late student loan applications are not guaranteed funding, you may lose a year of loan aid, if you take too long.

Keep in mind, you will not receive the first loan instalment until **three to four weeks after you have enrolled at college**. You should be prepared to live for the first two months at college, without loan money, as it won't arrive to your bank account until weeks after you've already started your studies.

FULL LISTING OF PROVINCIAL STUDENT LOAN AND FINANCIAL AID CONTACTS

Alberta Student Aid Alberta Service Centre Web: http://studentaid.alberta.ca Tel: 1-855-606-2096 (North America) 1-800 2 529-9242 (Outside North America) TTY: 1-855-306-2240	***Nunavut** Financial Assistance for Nunavut Students Web: http://gov.nu.ca/family-services/programs-services/financial-assistance-nunavut-students-fans Tel: 1-877-860-0680
British Columbia StudentAid BC Web: https://studentaidbc.ca/ Tel: 1-800-561-1818 (North America) 1-250-387-6100 (Outside North America	**Ontario** OSAP: Ontario Student Assistance Program Web: https://osap.gov.on.ca/OSAPPortal Tel: 807-343-7260 TTY: 1-800-465-3958
Manitoba Manitoba Student Aid Web: www.edu.gov.mb.ca/msa Tel: 1-800-204-1685 (North America) 204-945-6321 (Outside North America TTY: 204-945-8483 (within Manitoba) 1-866-209-0696 (within Canada/US)	**Prince Edward Island** Student Financial Services Web: http://www.studentloan.pe.ca/ Tel: 902-368-4640
New Brunswick Student Financial Services Web: www.studentaid.gnb.ca Tel: 1-800-667-5626 (North America) 506-453-2577 (Fredericton area)	***Quebec** Aide financière aux études (AFE) Web: http://www.afe.gouv.qc.ca/en/index.asp Tel: 1-877-643-3750 (North America) 418-643-3750
Newfoundland and Labrador Student Financial Services Web: http://www.aes.gov.nl.ca/studentaid/ Tel: 1-888-657-0800 (North America) 709-729-5849	**Saskatchewan** Saskatchewan Student Loans Web: http://www.saskatchewan.ca/studentloans Tel: 1-800-597-8278 (Within Canada) 306-787-5620
***Northwest Territories** Student Financial Assistance Web: http://www.nwtsfa.gov.nt.ca/ Tel: 1-800-661-0793 (North America) 867-873-7190	**Yukon** Student Financial Services Web: http://www.education.gov.yk.ca/ Tel: 1-800-661-0408 (Within Yukon) 867-667-5929

Nova Scotia Student Assistance Office Web: http://www.studentloans.ednet.ns.ca/ Tel: 1-800-565-8420 (Within Canada) 902-424-8420 TTY: 902-424-2058	** Nunavut, the Northwest Territories, and the province of Quebec, operate their own student assistance plans. If you are a resident of Nunavut, the Northwest Territories, or Quebec, contact the provincial or territorial student assistance office for further information.*

SUCCESSFUL APPLICATIONS

DIVERSITY IS YOUR FRIEND

No one factor will determine whether your application to a particular college is successful. All colleges take into account varying experiences, aptitudes, and achievements, in their assessments of student applications. Having top grades is important, but it's not the only factor, and sometimes it's not the most important factor.

Consider some of the following explanations from various universities, as to how they assess applications.

University of Washington—Tacoma campus

How are freshman applicants evaluated?

Applicants will be evaluated on a number of factors, including: grades and test scores; rigor of curriculum; activities and accomplishments; educational goals; diverse life experiences; and first generation college status. The factors are not of equal weight and no single factor will be sufficient to confer admission.

The University will offer admission to applicants who will most benefit from and contribute to the University's educational community. In selecting the freshman class, the University does not make admission decisions solely on the basis of past academic accomplishments. The intention is to enrol a freshman class that, as a whole, represents the diversity of our community.

http://www.tacoma.uw.edu/catalog/freshman-admission-requirements

University of California—Los Angeles (UCLA)

Freshman Selection - Fall 2016

Each year, UCLA considers many more excellent applicants for freshmen admission than it can possibly admit. The goal of the campus' admissions review process is to single out from a large and growing pool of academically strong applicants those unique individuals who have demonstrated the intellectual curiosity, tenacity, and commitment to community service expected of the UCLA graduate. These select applicants are the ones who would contribute the most to UCLA's dynamic learning environment; they are also the applicants who would make the most of being immersed in it. Although high school grade point average and standardized test scores are important indicators of academic achievement used in UCLA's admissions review, they only tell part of the story.

Admission Review Process

Selection is based on a comprehensive review of all information—both academic and personal—presented in the application. All applications are read twice, in their entirety, by professionally trained readers. After independently reading and analyzing a file, the reader determines a comprehensive score that is the basis upon which the student is ultimately admitted or denied. In addition, admissions managers conduct multiple checks for consistency and completeness throughout the reading process. While this evaluation process is based on human judgments rather than a system that quantifies factors and incorporates them into a numerical formula, the extensive reader training, comprehensive reading of files, as well as other monitoring procedures, ensure that the process is highly reliable. Formal tests of reliability are conducted regularly to assure quality control.

The admission review reflects the readers' thoughtful consideration of the full spectrum of the applicant's qualifications, based on all evidence provided in the application, and viewed in the context of the applicant's academic and personal circumstances and the overall strength of the UCLA applicant pool. Using a broad concept of merit, readers employ the following criteria which carry no pre-assigned weights:

1. The applicant's full record of achievement in college preparatory work in high school;
2. Personal qualities of the applicant;
3. Likely contributions to the intellectual and cultural vitality of the campus;
4. Performance on standardized tests, including the ACT plus Writing or SAT Reasoning, and any Advanced Placement or International Baccalaureate Higher Level examinations the applicant may have taken;
5. Achievement in academic enrichment programs, including, but not limited to, those sponsored by the University of California;
6. Other evidence of achievement. This criterion will recognize exemplary, sustained achievement in any field of intellectual or creative endeavor; accomplishments in the performing arts and athletics; employment; leadership in school or community organizations or activities; and community service;
7. Opportunities. All achievements, both academic and non-academic, are considered in the context of the opportunities an applicant has had, and the reader's assessment is based on how fully the applicant has taken advantage of those opportunities;
8. Challenges. For an applicant who has faced any hardships or unusual circumstances, readers consider the maturity, determination, and insight with which he or she has responded to and/or overcome them. Readers also consider other contextual factors that bear directly on the applicant's achievement, including linguistic background, parental education level, and other indicators of support available in the home.

Adapted from www.admissions.ucla.edu/Prospect/Adm_fr/FrSel.htm

APPLICATION MATERIALS

Every college will differ as to which specific materials they require for their application procedures. The success of your application will hinge on a combined consideration of the following items:

ACADEMIC RECORD

Your academic record consists of all of your grades, from Grade 9 onward. Generally, all your grades will appear in one transcript (from your junior high/high school) or on multiple transcripts, if you have attended multiple junior highs and high schools. In applying, make sure to obtain transcripts from all the schools you attended since Grade 9.

HIGH SCHOOL COURSE LOAD

Colleges and universities want to make sure that, if you have high grades, it's not because you took half as many courses as your colleagues. Conversely, if your grades are not as high as those of other candidates, but you can demonstrate your course load was heavier (i.e. you took more courses and covered more curricular content), your application may not suffer. Demonstration of a heavy course load is in your benefit, as it indicates that you are able to handle the heavy workload associated with university academics.

DIFFICULTY OF YOUR COURSE LOAD

You may have a plethora of credits appearing on your transcript—in fact, you may have many more credits than are required by your provincial government to graduate from high school. If your courses are composed of less difficult academic options, (i.e. basic mathematics as opposed to calculus, or regular-stream biology as opposed to I.B. biology) the university will take this into account. If your grades are lower because you took a full-I.B. (International Baccalaureate) or a full-AP (Advanced Placement) course load, the colleges will acknowledge that fact and weigh the difficulty of your courses.

Class rank

Every high school varies, in terms of its curriculum delivery, teaching staff, and standards of evaluation, college and university admissions staff recognize that an A+ at one school is not the same as an A+ at another school. So colleges and universities will often look at your "class rank." At some high schools, class rank is indicated on your transcript; at other schools, it's not. Therefore, you should always ask your academic referees (i.e. the teacher, or teachers, who write academic reference letters for you) to include a note in their letter stating how you rank among your peers, within particular courses. If you rank high (e.g. you are in the top 10 in your graduating class) this will benefit your application immensely.

Standardized test scores

The vast majority of colleges and universities require a test score, for either the SAT (Standard Reasoning Test) or the ACT (American College Test). Some colleges do not require standardized test scores, but they may recommend you submit scores if you can (and you always should).

Application essay

The application essay is a piece of writing you produce specifically for your college application form. The college you are applying to will specify an application question (the question usually changes every year). If you are applying through the Common Application System, that application will specify one, or more, options for your application essay. The admissions officers will judge the quality of your composition, style, word choice, and use of examples, to determine whether your essay is worthy of university admission. Note that admissions officers also look to your application essay as an indication of your personality traits. If you are applying to a particular liberal arts college, your application essay will need to demonstrate that you fit the specific kind of student profile the college is looking to populate its campus with.

Extra-curricular activities

Your extra-curricular activities are an important part of your college application. They indicate your ability to engage in social and academic activities, outside of that which is required of you in your classes. You want to emphasize the leadership, teamwork, management, and organizational aspects of your extra-curricular activities. If your activities include the fine arts or sports, you may want to emphasize the particular talents those activities have helped you to develop (e.g. the ability to play the flute, read musical script, or captain a team), especially if you plan to continue those activities at the college level.

Extra-curricular activities can include (but are not restricted to) the following:

- debating club
- public-speaking club
- student government (e.g. student council)
- extra-curricular language groups (e.g. French club)
- sports teams
- musical groups
- artistic groups (e.g. Painting and sculpting club)
- dance groups
- drama groups and theatre
- conference-organizing activities
- volunteering in community organizations
- peer tutoring and counseling

Teacher and counsellor recommendations

Your teachers and counsellors will serve as your academic referees. They will be the ones that write recommendation letters you are required to submit with your application. Remember, academic referees are busy people, especially at application time. They will probably be writing many reference letters for a number of students at the same time. So help your referees! Write a list of things you think are strong traits about yourself, or things you've achieved at school, which you would like your referee(s) to mention in their letter(s). Don't be shy about this process; you need to advocate for yourself. Provide your referees with your list of items, ask them to consider mentioning some or all of those traits and achievements, especially if you believe those items will help your application. Your referees will thank you. It is hard to remember all the things that even great students do!

ADMISSIONS INTERVIEW

Many of the Ivy Leagues schools, and liberal arts colleges, require personal interviews as part of their application process. Often times, schools will abrogate the need for a personal interview if you are an international applicant. Make sure to check your college's admission guideline to determine whether you have to travel to the school, or meet with a local representative of the school's alumni.

For those schools that do not require a personal interview, you should still request one, assuming it's physically possible for you to meet with one of the school's local representatives. Interviews are an excellent way of establishing a sense of who you are; they help to leave a lasting impression. Rarely are interviews used as a means of disqualifying student applicants. Rather, they are used as a means of determining between students whose applications are equally weighted in all other matters.

STANDARD APPLICATION MATERIALS—BE PREPARED!

In addition to the usual considerations stated in the previous section, there are a number of standard items that will appear in almost every college application package. If you're looking to prepare ahead of time, here's what you can expect:

APPLICATION FORM

As we saw with the Princeton University example provided earlier, each college will specify which application form(s) it wants you to use. Sometimes the college will have one specific application form; at other times, as with Princeton, students can use the online **Common Application Form**, which hundreds of colleges in the U.S. use as a standardized admittance form.

In the past, students had to obtain paper copies of these forms, then submit hand-written, or typewritten, forms back to the college. Although those options still exist, nowadays most colleges offer their application forms online, in both Word and PDF formats, so now you can download the form and fill it in using your computer.

APPLICATION FEE

You will often be asked to pay an application fee, which in Spring 2015 was on average $41 per application. If you're planning on applying to multiple colleges, this could run up quite a bill. The fee is, almost always, non-refundable. On the plus side, some colleges charge no fee.

High school transcript

All colleges ask for an account of your grades, usually from Grade 9 onward. If you live in a province where high school begins at Grade 10, you will have to contact your junior high school to get your junior high transcript sent to the appropriate colleges.

Usually the **transcript request form** will be sent to you as part of your application package (you receive an application package in the post, once you have expressed interest in applying to a particular school via your counselling office, sports club, college fair, or by requesting application information directly from the college online). Have your high school counsellor help you complete the request form and submit it promptly to ensure timely delivery of your grades.

Grade Point Average Conversion Table

Colleges will convert your junior/high school grades into a "Grade Point Equivalent" (GPA) in order to rank you with other applicants. Below is a general guide, to GPA equivalences, for junior/high school grades offered as percentages.

Grade GPA			
60 2.0	70 3.0	80 3.5	90 4.0
61 2.1	71 3.0	81 3.5	91 4.0
62 2.2	72 3.0	82 3.5	92 4.0
63 2.3	73 3.0	83 3.5	93 4.0
64 2.4	74 3.0	84 3.5	94 4.0
65 2.5	75 3.0	85 3.5	95 4.0
66 2.6	76 3.1	86 3.7	96 4.0
67 2.7	77 3.2	87 3.7	97 4.0
68 2.8	78 3.3	88 3.7	98 4.0
69 2.9	79 3.4	89 3.7	99 4.0
			100 4.0

Note that this is a general guide only. The admissions staff at your college will be able to tell you exactly what your GPA will convert to based on the college's specific conversion tables.

Admission test scores

The SAT Reasoning Test, the ACT College Test, and SAT Subject Tests are often required as part of your application package. Make sure you've prepared early and have registered for, and written, the exam(s) (with time to spare).

Letters of recommendation

Colleges will sometimes ask for up to 5 letters of recommendation from teachers, sports coaches, community leaders, and volunteering associates. Prepare a list of potential letter-writers, and make sure to let those people know you might need them to write a letter on your behalf. Depending on the college and/or particular scholarship applications, you may only need some of those reference letters. It's always good to have too many than too few people who are willing to write supporting documents for you. To ensure you have strong letters of recommendation, discuss the college requirements, and profile, with your letter-writers ahead of time, and indicate to them those things about your academic, sporting, volunteering, or personal history you would like mentioned in the letter.

The Essay

Many private colleges require a "personal essay" or "personal statement" that describes who you are and what your primary objectives in life are. These essays can seem difficult to write, especially given they should help set your application apart from everyone else's. Some basic rules to follow in producing a top quality essay include the following:

College Application Essay

You can find more advice on writing your college application essay by consulting the following resources:

The College Application Essay, by Sarah Myers McGinty, published by Collegeboard.org (updated annually).

How to Get Into the Top Colleges, by Richard Montauk and Krista Klein, published by Penguin Group (2009).

a) Be specific

A generic essay that talks about abstract and undefined concepts such as "I want to improve myself," "I want to contribute to the community," or "I want to be a leader" will not impress admissions teams. If those sentiments do in fact reflect how you feel about yourself, or your upcoming college experience, you need to make them concrete, by offering detailed and specific examples about what you've done in the past or what you plan to do at college, to justify your sentiments. Whether you choose to write an essay that highlights personal goals and objectives or one that discusses a general theme (i.e. as chosen by the college or Common Application), providing **detailed examples** is the best means of setting your essay apart from everyone else's.

RULE: ***Avoid generalizations; offer specifics.***

b) Clean copy

Always be sure to edit, re-edit, and edit your essay one more time before you submit it as part of your application. Remember, no matter how many times you read your own essay, you will miss some grammatical and syntactical points. Always have a parent, friend, counsellor, or teacher proofread your *final* copy before submitting it.

RULE: ***Everyone needs an editor; get one!***

c) Follow the rules

If an application says "200 words," only write two hundred words. Don't think you are above the rules governing applications. At best, extra words will simply be ignored; at worst, admissions staff will take it as an indication that you don't follow academic standards when they are stipulated. Do not do yourself a disservice. Follow the rules stipulated by the application, and do not write more or less than what is required of you.

There is one caveat to this rule. If an application suggests a range—say "300 to 500 words"—always aim for the upper end of the range, but do not exceed it. In such instances, it is in your benefit to write 499 words about yourself or about the essay topic. If you can include one extra example to highlight your point or solidify your argument, then do so.

RULE: ***Word lengths are non-negotiable; aim for the upper limit.***

SAMPLE APPLICATION ESSAY

The following essay is an example of a successful college entrance essay.

Typical College Application Essay Questions

No two colleges are the same when it comes to posing application essay questions. But because the application process is such a grand and universalizing one, there are some typical types of questions you will see posed on your application.

Start to think about how you would go about answering such questions. In preparing your thoughts, keep in mind that these essays are like all other essays that you write for high school, even if they are about "personal experience." In other words, they must have **an introduction, a body,** and **a conclusion**.

Here is a list of some real college application essay questions; they demonstrate typical question types:

- Describe your most rewarding or unrewarding educational experience.
- Ask and answer your own question.
- How do you envision your freshman year?
- Write a page of your own autobiography.
- Discuss an issue of personal, local, national, or international concern and its importance to you.
- Indicate a person who has had a significant influence on you and describe that influence.
- How do you see the world in 2020?
- Describe how a song, poem, piece of art, book, etc., influenced your life.
- Select two ideals listed in our literature and relate them to your personal beliefs and convictions.
- Evaluate a significant experience or achievement that has special meaning to you.
- How have you taken something you've learned in the class room and integrated it into your non-academic life?
- If you could meet anyone, real or imaginary, who would it be?
- How will your knowledge of other cultures affect your studies?
- Describe a situation in which your values were challenged.
- Pick a recent event and relate it to a turning point in your life.
- Describe an experience that illustrates a proverb, maxim, or quote that has special meaning for you?
- Relate your future goals to studying at our school.

The student has offered the admissions officers an essay that is well-structured and well-edited. Some aspects of the writing could be improved upon, but overall the piece contains clear and distinct examples, which give the reader a sense of the student's overall capacities and potential for success.

This student was editor-in-chief of his high school newspaper and was aiming for a career in law. He applied to Harvard University.

Essay question: Evaluate a significant experience or achievement that has special meaning to you.

I blew out a tire today. I was driving home from a football team dinner, perhaps a bit too fast, and a small black cat with shining yellow eyes darted out in front of the car. I swerved. I hit the curb. I heard a pop. I knew I was in trouble. I turned carefully onto the first side street, an unlit, unmarked roadway deep in a town I had never previously visited, and went to size up the damage after seeing those brilliant yellow eyes run safely off the other side of the road. Three gaping holes large enough to fit my fist through were visible—though only as jagged edged shapes even darker than the black wall of the tire—in the dim light cast by the bulb of the open car door. I was walking quite briskly towards the gas station I had passed, now about a hundred feet away, when I stopped myself to collect my thoughts.

As I saw it, the easy answer was only a few feet away. I could simply have walked to the gas station, bestowed my mother's credit card and my problem upon some else, and have gotten my tire changed. I imagined doing this, however, and found the picture in my mind to be quite distasteful. I saw myself as the quintessential child of privilege, talented and independent in the classroom, perhaps, but helpless as far as completing one of those random and menial challenges that life finds it necessary to confer upon us. So I stopped and stood for a moment, feeling strangely empty in the bare light of a street lamp on Main Street in Dover, before deciding that I would change the tire myself.

Though there is no differential calculus involved in changing a tire, I still found the task to be quite difficult and quite humbling; it requires persistence, along with elbow grease of the most literal sort. After I managed to find the spare tire buried in the Volvo's trunk, I started the dirty task of finding the oil-slicked, sooty place in the undercarriage where the jack attaches to the car. Eventually, I managed to jack the car up, and I removed the busted tire with relative ease. I hit my first "roadblock" when I tried to install the spare. There was a small metal piece on the wheel base which apparently must be lined up with a pea-sized hole in the tire hub, but it took me almost ten minutes to see this metal guide and take appropriate action. So I tried, without success, to simply put the tire on the axle; I was trying to put it on backwards numerous times, dropping it on my own feet often, and becoming more and more frustrated all the while. Suddenly the irony of the situation hit me. Here I am, with grease on my hands and slacks, still wearing my prep-school uniform of shirt and tie, trying to do something which all the classroom time in the world could never possibly teach me.

I have long known that education is not confined to the classroom. So as I sat waiting for a replacement tire at National Tire and Battery—pondering my situation and watching Jeopardy—I realised that part of what makes me a good student is that I do not only learn in class. My private school education may have directly helped me to know that the correct response to the 600 dollar answer in category "B" was "What is Bora-Bora?", but less than a little of what I truly know has come from academic lectures. I read voraciously on a wide range of topics, I do crossword puzzles every day, and I am often late for upcoming classes because I spend ten minutes after the previous one engaging the teacher in a more in-depth conversation. Even beyond academic pursuits, though, I have learned physical and mental toughness from football and wrestling, I have learned about leadership and journalism from my position on the newspaper, and I have learned much about expression and emotion from music and guitar. I even dropped Homer Simpson in favour of District Attorney Jack McCoy once I figured out how much I could learn from watching "Law and Order" on NBC. In fact, every dimension of my character and each event of my life is an invisible classroom, and so whether I am changing a tire or organizing Holocaust readings at school, I am learning and growing. Accepting the challenges of school and difficult courses is still extremely important to me, but accepting the challenges that life presents can be just as educational and equally important.

Adapted from How to Get Into the Top Colleges (2006), by Richard Montauk and Krista Klein. Prentice Hall Press (New York, NY).

Interview

Many colleges, especially private ones, will request an interview as part of your application process; if you live far from the college campus, you may be asked to connect with a local alumni of the college. You should practise being interviewed ahead of time. Ask friends and family to run mock interviews with you, make sure you know as much about the student profile of the particular college as possible. Certain colleges, like Yale or Harvard, will seek out people they feel fit the Yale or Harvard "vision." Make sure you know what that vision is, and try to think of ways you fit into the kind of community the college is trying to build.

Audition and Portfolios

For degree applicants in music, theatre, drama, and the fine arts (and sometimes for literature or creative writing degree applicants), colleges will request portfolios of work, demonstrating your capacities and range of work. Be prepared to put together a portfolio if you are considering such a degree.

See sample Admissions Essays at the back of this book!

THE COMMON APPLICATION

The **Common Application membership association** was established in 1975 by 15 private colleges that sought to provide a common, standardized, first-year application form for use by any member institution. The Common Application is a not-for-profit membership organization that has committed itself to providing reliable services that promote equity, access, and integrity in the college application process.

The organization states its overall mission is *"To serve students, member institutions, and secondary schools by providing applications—online and in print—that students and school officials may submit to any of our nearly 400 members. [The Common Application] promotes access by evaluating students using a holistic selection process."*

The Common Application is now a standard entry application used by colleges (both public and private) across the U.S. The number of colleges and universities using the **Common Application** now numbers over 400, and that number represents the full range of higher educational institutions. You can find the Common Application at the following web address:

http://www.commonapp.org/

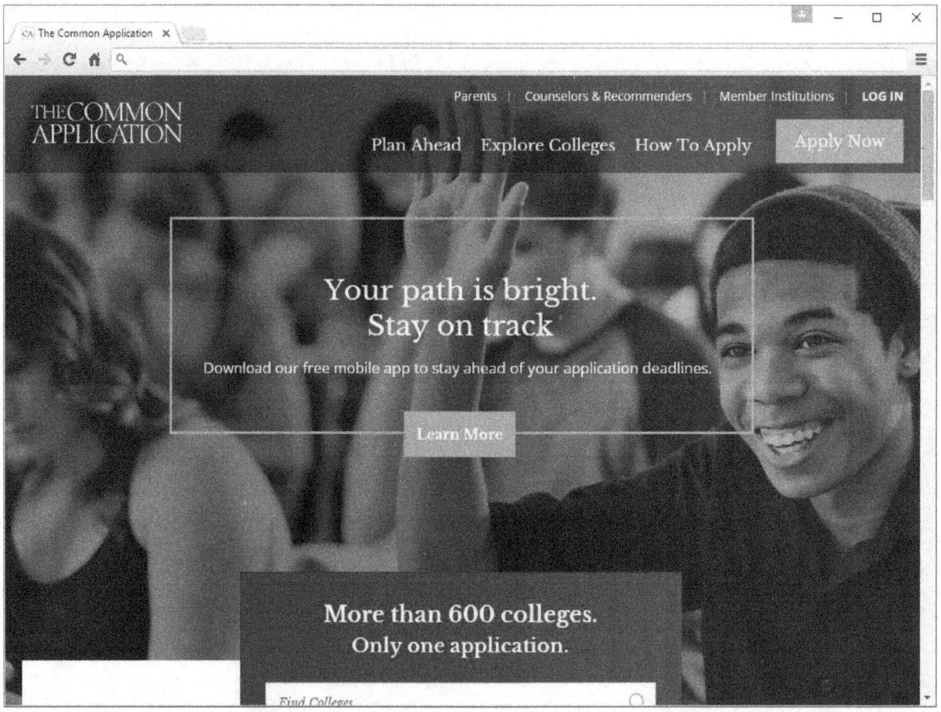

Common Application Member Institutions

The Common Application members are located in the U.S. and the District of Columbia, as well as in France, Germany, Italy, United Kingdom, and Switzerland. A complete alphabetical list of colleges and universities, that have chosen to use the Common Application as a means of promoting holistic entrance applications, can be found at the following web address: http://www.commonapp.org/member-institutions

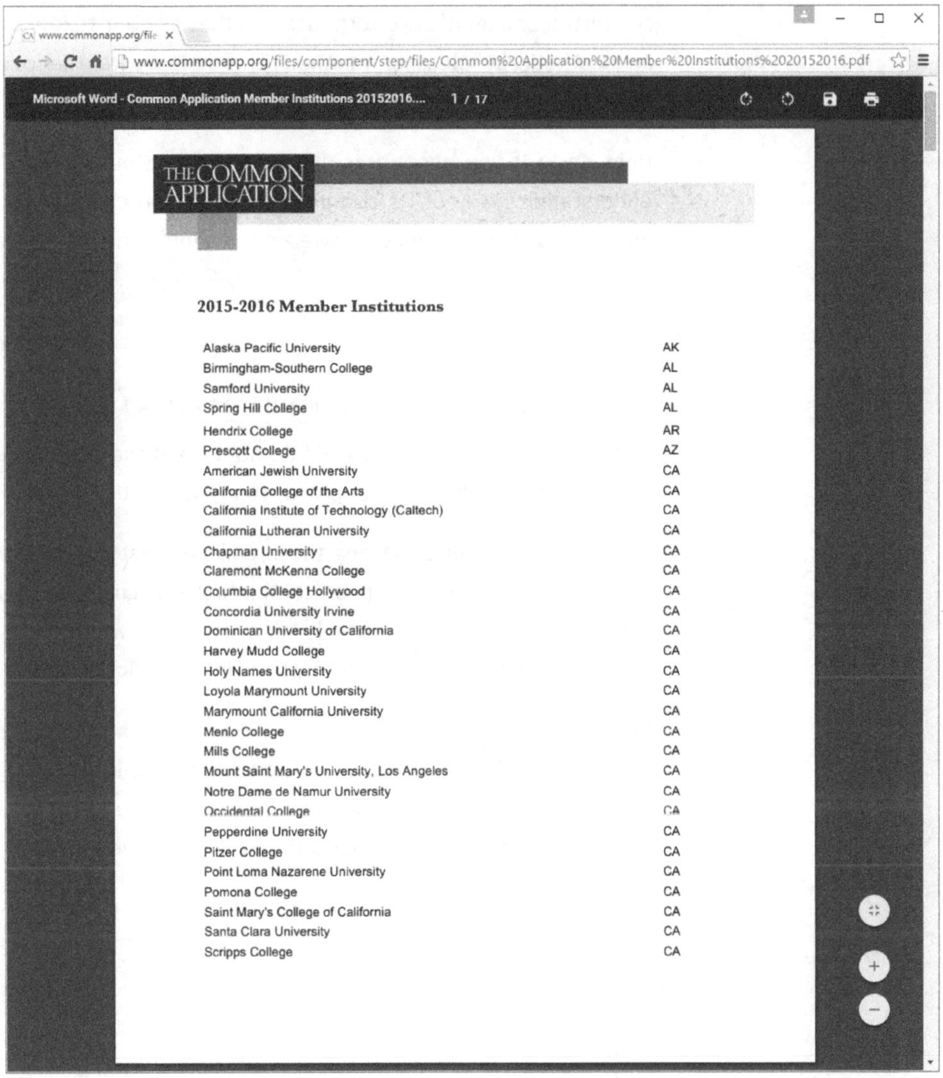

2015-2016 Member Institutions

Alaska Pacific University	AK
Birmingham-Southern College	AL
Samford University	AL
Spring Hill College	AL
Hendrix College	AR
Prescott College	AZ
American Jewish University	CA
California College of the Arts	CA
California Institute of Technology (Caltech)	CA
California Lutheran University	CA
Chapman University	CA
Claremont McKenna College	CA
Columbia College Hollywood	CA
Concordia University Irvine	CA
Dominican University of California	CA
Harvey Mudd College	CA
Holy Names University	CA
Loyola Marymount University	CA
Marymount California University	CA
Menlo College	CA
Mills College	CA
Mount Saint Mary's University, Los Angeles	CA
Notre Dame de Namur University	CA
Occidental College	CA
Pepperdine University	CA
Pitzer College	CA
Point Loma Nazarene University	CA
Pomona College	CA
Saint Mary's College of California	CA
Santa Clara University	CA
Scripps College	CA

There are certain reasons why the Common Application is a preferred option for both students and universities. Conversely, there are some reasons why you may consider not using the Common Application.

Benefits of the Common Application

One application, many universities: The most obvious benefit to the Common Application is that you only have to fill in the pages of basic information (such as name, birth date, high school information, address, etc.) once, rather than multiple times for different colleges.

Standardized format and readability: The Common Application is filled out online and is submitted online. It's pre-formatted so that all your text lines up properly, and prints in an aesthetically pleasing manner. This helps with the overall presentation of your application.

Help desk: If you encounter difficulty in filling out in the Common Application, or in understanding any of its component parts, you can contact the Common Application office and get your queries answered in a timely and direct manner.

Disadvantages of the Common Application

Not universal: Many colleges still do not accept the Common Application. Depending on the colleges you choose to apply to, you may end up filling in multiple applications.

Going the extra mile: Among those colleges that do accept the Common Application, there is usually the option of completing the college's individual application. Often, admissions staff look favourably upon students who go the extra mile and fill in the college's own application, thereby showing specific interest in that particular college.

Extra materials: Many colleges—including all of the Ivy Leagues schools and many liberal arts colleges—require additional (i.e. supplemental) application materials to be submitted along with the Common Application. If you fail to complete the supplemental application material, your application will be deemed invalid.

Early Decision (ED) vs. Early Action (EA)

Early decision refers to early applications that are submitted to the colleges and decided upon, well before the final deadline for yearly applications. Early decision application deadlines are usually in November of each year. These applications are judged by December of the same year.

Restrictions for early decision (ED) include the following:

- You can only apply for early decision to a single school. You can apply for early action (EA) [see below] and regular admission to other schools.
- Early decision constitutes a binding contract—meaning, if you are accepted to your early decision school, you must withdraw all your other applications, including any that you may have made to Canadian and British universities!
- Because early decision is binding upon applicants, students should only apply using the early decision process to a particular college if they are 100 percent certain they want to attend that school.

Why apply for early decision?

Early decision applicants demonstrate their keen interest in one particular school. For colleges (such as the Ivy League schools), which seek to deliver particular student profiles, early decision applicants may be favoured, so far as they meet the other criteria of entry.

The early decision process indicates to the college that you are set on attending that particular school, as opposed to just including it as one of the other multiple schools you are applying to.

Early action (EA) refers to early applications (usually submitted in November) that are decided upon early (usually by December).

Characteristics of early action (EA) include the following:

- Early action is not binding. Even if you are accepted early, you can still wait to hear from the other schools to which you have applied, before making your decision.
- You may apply to more than one school using the early action process, unless the college stipulates that it is a "single choice early action" (SCEA) school, in which case you can only apply to that school.
- Early action is less risky than early decision (ED), because it's not binding.

APPLYING TO TOP COLLEGES

Who are the admissions officers?

All colleges have admissions departments composed of various admissions officers. Those officers (i.e. staff members) travel around the United States, and internationally, throughout the year to advertise their respective schools to potential students.

The job of the admissions officer is to publicize their schools and to generate a high number of applicants, on a yearly basis.

By the time November rolls around, admissions officers form into a number of admissions committees. Those committees read through application, as well as the thousands of other incoming applications, in order to decide who gets in and who gets denied entry.

The multiple roles of admission officers

In their committees, admissions officers look to do more than just decide who gets in.

Admissions is a process that is as much about building reputation and identity for colleges as it is about granting entry to applicants.

SELECTIVITY

Many of the top schools in the U.S., and especially private colleges (including the Ivy League schools), look to maintain a certain college profile. A college's admissions statistics play a large role in building that profile. Admissions statistics play a large role in determining which applications are successful and which applications are not.

Admissions statistics include data such as the following:

1. Acceptance rates versus application rates (i.e. how many people get accepted compared to how many people apply).

2. Matriculation rates versus acceptance rates (i.e. how many of the successful applicants accept the offer and chose to attend the school).

3. SAT/ACT average entry scores (i.e. the average score among accepted students).

4. High school class rank average entry positions (i.e. the average graduating rank of accepted students).

5. Demographic spread (i.e. how many accepted students come from the college's host state, other states, and other countries).

6. Socio-economic spread (i.e. how many accepted students come from low-income families).

UNDERSTANDING SELECTIVITY

The first four of the admissions statistics listed, on the previous page, play to a college's identity as selective and elite.

Admissions officers hope for large numbers of incoming applicants so the college's acceptance rate is low. The more applications a school receives, the more candidates it gets to turn down. As a result, colleges with high application rates, but low acceptance rates, appear more selective than colleges with higher acceptance rates.

These selectivity rates are part of a college's marketing strategy. They are not necessarily reflective of the quality of education that a student will be receiving. In terms of public perception, selectivity often insinuates elite standards or a sense that the school is a "top" school because it is hard to get into.

Have no doubt—colleges like to foster this perception because it's in their financial interest to do so. The more selective they are, the more sought after they become. This, in turn, allows top colleges to set their tuition rates higher than other less selective schools. Ivy League colleges, for example, will encourage applications from all sorts of students, including those the admissions officers know will not be successful, because it drives the college's acceptance rate lower.

Students should be aware of these marketing techniques before applying to college. It's for this reason that finding the right fit is more important than applying everywhere (the latter of which is both a time-consuming and expensive route to take).

COLLEGE COMPOSITE

Colleges are not only interested in individual applicants, but also in the composition of their overall student bodies. This is known as the college's composite.

Particular colleges—especially private liberal arts colleges and the Ivy League schools—seek to portray themselves as the home of diverse communities. College admissions officers usually privilege applications from students who can portray special or unique talents. Your ethnic background, religious background, geographical origin, linguistic abilities, travel experience, work experience, and sporting, musical, and theatrical abilities will play a role in identifying you as a diverse candidate in the eyes of admissions officers.

As a Canadian applicant, you have the advantage of being an international student. Many elite colleges will set a quota for international applicants, in order to add to the international diversity of their campuses.

NEED CONSCIOUSNESS

One of the most important diversifying factors admission staff consider is an applicant's financial background. Many top colleges look to admit a certain number of students who cannot afford tuition rates.

Over the past decade, the need to democratize higher education and render college studies accessible to low-income and gifted students has become a prominent theme within pedagogical and educational circles in the United States.

Thus, colleges have developed need conscious models so as to accept high achieving students who hail from poor financial backgrounds.

SUMMARY OF NEED CONSIDERATIONS

NEED-BLIND

Whether you can pay the tuition or not does not factor into your application assessment.

NEED-AWARE

One of the factors working for or against your application is whether your family can afford the full tuition at the college.

NEED-BLIND ADMISSIONS

Many top colleges, and especially the Ivy League private colleges, can boast large endowment funds, which allow them to admit applicants based on the applicant's academic and extra-curricular merits.

Applicants to need-blind colleges are admitted according to standard admissions procedures. After being admitted, if it turns out that the student cannot afford the tuition, the college will offer the student a financial package that is based on a thorough assessment of the applicant's finances.

Each college uses its own algorithm to determine how much money an admitted student will receive. Those financial packages will take the form of (non-repayable) grants, (repayable) student loans, and on-campus job opportunities.

In some instances, colleges might offer full, or near-full, tuition aid. Depending on your parents' financial status. The college may expect you to pay a certain portion of your fees.

NEED-AWARE ADMISSIONS

Not all colleges have enough money in endowment funds to pay for student tuition. The admissions procedures at these schools are labelled need-aware or need conscious.

Based on this model, admissions officers will consider whether a student is able to pay his or her tuition fees. If you can pay for your tuition, your application is looked upon more favourably. At many colleges, those students with high financial needs are placed at the bottom of the selection list, despite what might be high academic performance or laudable extra-curricular qualifications.

Generally, a student's financial requirements only become a determining factor near the bottom of the acceptance list, at which point, admissions staff looks to accept only a final few applicants.

Oftentimes, if you are a top student (i.e. one who possesses all the desirable qualities a college may be looking for), your financial background will not factor into your application assessment, even at need-aware colleges.

However, if your application is one of the weaker ones, your financial background will play a role in determining whether you, or someone who has more money, ultimately gets accepted.

Need-Assessment Case Study: Harvard College

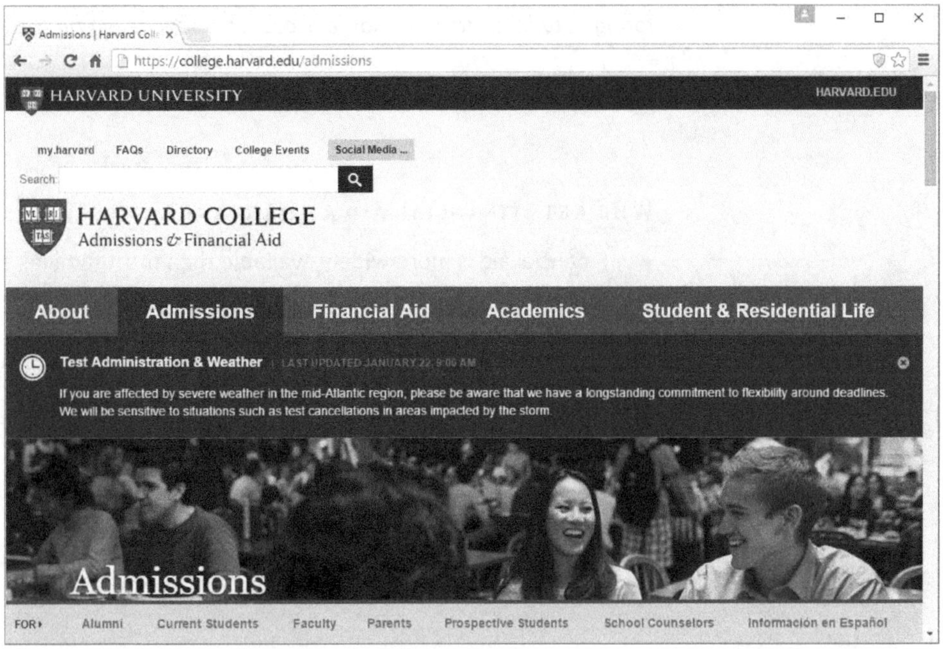

General points to consider for Harvard admissions

- Harvard College does not award merit scholarships of any kind (not all Ivy League schools are like this, but merit scholarships are small—this is the opposite in Canada).
- 70% of Harvard students receive some form of financial aid-grant, loan and/or part-time work.
- Harvard's policy of need-based financial aid is designed to meet 100% of a family's demonstrated need.
- Harvard's financial aid policies apply equally to international students and to U.S. citizens.

NEED-BLINDNESS AT HARVARD

- Admission to Harvard is need-blind—a lack of financial resources, and need for financial aid, is not detriment to a student's admission.

Harvard states:

"Applying for financial aid does not jeopardize a student's chances for admission, and foreign students have the same access to financial aid funding as do U.S. citizens."

WHO GETS FINANCIAL AID AT HARVARD?

- Financial aid is more widely available than most families expect.
- "Need" is based on a variety of family circumstances, not income alone. Even families with annual incomes exceeding $150,000 (U.S.) may qualify for scholarship aid, depending on how many children are in the family, and other financial obligations.
- Harvard adjusts individual financial aid packages to accommodate significant changes in a family's financial situation over the years (students must reapply for financial assistance each year).

COLLEGE LOAN OPTIONS AT HARVARD

- Students from foreign countries may receive loans from the Harvard Loan Program, as a part of their financial aid package.
- No interest accrues on those loans during full-time enrolment in college or graduate school, or for six months thereafter.
- Students must begin to repay these loans six months after the end of full-time enrolment in college or graduate school.

JOBS AT HARVARD

- A job is not required as part of an international student's financial aid package, but is easily available.
- All students, international or American, who demonstrate financial need will be offered a modest loan or job as part of their financial aid.
- Some students choose to take a loan for the full amount, others will choose to work for the full amount, with a job requiring about twelve hours per week, others will choose to have a combination of loan and job.
- Jobs are plentiful and are often interesting and relevant to academic interests.

TYPICAL AID PACKAGE AT HARVARD

- For international students who qualified for financial aid for the 2015-2016 academic year, an average aid package included a job offer and a financial scholarship.
- Keep in mind that 2015-2016 fees for tuition, room, board, insurance, and personal expenses totaled approximately from $65,000 to $70,000 USD.
- For the 2015-2016 academic year, parents with total incomes of less than $65,000 USD were not expected to pay for any of their child's/children's tuition and academic fees. This amounted to approximately 20% of the Harvard parent community.

THE "RECESSION" AND YOUR COLLEGE APPLICATION

As a result of dwindling endowment investments over the years of recessionary contraction, many colleges are now adopting need-aware procedures.

Some Ivy League colleges, such as Harvard, have stated publicly that their aim is to remain need-blind. However, decreased endowment funds, increased operating costs, and decreased student applicant numbers mean that even rich colleges, such as Harvard, are reassessing the liberality of their financial aid packages.

In the new economic climate, some colleges are deliberating a policy whereby only top applicants would receive need-blind assessment, while those further down the list would be assessed using need-aware procedures. Students who have demonstrated financial need, and who require financial help to pay their tuition fees, will need to work harder to make sure they are among the top applicants.

To find out whether your college of choice is altering its admissions procedures, in light of the past years of global economic contraction, make sure to check its admissions website. In the "Questions and Answers" or "FAQs" section of the college's admissions site, you will be able to find out whether admissions procedures are need-aware or whether they are becoming need-aware in the near future.

Colleges Accepting More

www.nytimes.com/2009/03/31/education/31college.html?_r=0

SECTIONS HOME SEARCH The New York Times SUBSCRIBE NOW LOG IN

EDUCATION

Paying in Full as the Ticket Into Colleges

By KATE ZERNIKE MARCH 30, 2009

Email Share Tweet Save More

In the bid for a fat envelope this year, it may help, more than usual, to have a fat wallet.

Facing fallen endowments and needier students, many colleges are looking more favorably on wealthier applicants as they make their admissions decisions this year.

Institutions that have pledged to admit students regardless of need are finding ways to increase the number of those who pay the full cost in ways that allow the colleges to maintain the claim of being need-blind — taking more students from the transfer or waiting lists, for instance, or admitting more foreign students who pay full tuition.

Private colleges that acknowledge taking financial status into account say they are even more aware of that factor this year.

"If you are a student of means or ability, or both, there has never been a better year," said Robert A. Sevier, an enrollment consultant to colleges.

How Well Do You Know Air Force One?

Score 0

Despite its integral role in the 1997 film "Air Force One," the real plane doesn't have an escape pod

TRUE FALSE

1 2 3 4 5 6 7 8 9 10

Waiting for match.basebanner.com...

GENERAL ADMISSIONS EVALUATION CRITERIA

There are three general characteristics that admissions officers will look at as they review your application.

ACADEMIC AND INTELLECTUAL POTENTIAL

The academic potential, of any given candidate, is judged on the following criteria:

- high school transcripts (Grades 9 – 12)
- high school profile
- standardized test scores
- recommendation/referee letters
- written application
- interview

Colleges are looking for applicants who can demonstrate high grades and high scores. Schools will also look favourably upon students whose grades improve substantially over the years.

Colleges will not look favourably upon students whose grades have dropped off over the years, unless there are extenuating circumstances (e.g. the death of a parent) to explain the score discrepancy.

NON-ACADEMIC PURSUITS AND TALENTS

The non-academic talents, of any given candidate, are judged using the following components of an application:

- written application
- interview
- recommendation/referee letters

Colleges want to know what you do in your time outside the classroom. The non-academic pursuits you highlight in your application ultimately depend upon the particular college(s) you are applying to.

If you are applying to an engineering or mathematics program at M.I.T., you should highlight your talents in music, fine arts, linguistics, international travel and community volunteering in order to distinguish yourself from every other math whiz out there.

If, on the other hand, you are applying to a liberal arts college, such as Amherst, you should highlight the fact that you are a member of the science and mathematics club, or that you volunteer as a science tutor for other students, in order to distinguish yourself from every other writing genius and political guru out there.

In other words, use your non-academic pursuits and talents to set yourself apart from the typical type of student applying to your college of choice.

Personal Attributes

The personal attributes, of any given candidate, are judged based upon the candidate's:

- Written application
- Interview
- Recommendation/referee letters

Colleges determine the personal attributes of applicants based upon the manner in which they describe both their academic and non-academic pursuits.

There are some typical attributes college admissions staff are looking to glean from your application materials. Those attributes include the following:

- passion
- perseverance
- compassion
- interpersonal skills
- creativity
- maturity
- honesty
- curiosity

You do not need to demonstrate you possess a little bit of all of these qualities, as colleges are looking for well-rounded classes, not well-rounded individuals. It's best to focus on a few of your best attributes, by using your extracurricular pursuits to highlight specific attributes, especially if you think they will set you apart from other applicants.

As Richard Montauk and Krista Klein argue in *How to Get Into the Top Colleges* (2006):

"The most successful applicants are those who can prove to the admissions committees that their excellence—attained in as few as one, two, or three areas—will allow them to better contribute to and benefit from an education at a top college than other applicants would."

UNDERSTANDING FIT

All the considerations stipulated on previous page must be understood within the general context of a college's culture or fit. Students must sculpt their applications to demonstrate both uniqueness and fit.

These two aspects of the college admissions procedure may seem paradoxical, but they aren't. Colleges want to find unique students, but only in so far as those students match their local cultures. In other words, if you are applying to M.I.T., it probably isn't because you want to specialise in fine arts and theatre. You need to pick your college(s) according to the strengths that the college demonstrates. First, determine which program a given college advertises as its flagship program (e.g. engineering and mathematics at M.I.T. or creative writing and classics at Amherst). Then determine whether that is the right fit for you. If it's not, you need to keep looking at other colleges to determine where you fit best.

TIMELINE FOR SUCCESS

Grade 10

- Register for, and write, the PSAT.
- Start getting involved in school organizations and activities to bolster your curriculum vitae and future application.
- Focus on your grades and make sure to achieve the highest marks you can—remember, American universities will look at all your marks from Grade 9 onwards!
- Start searching for scholarship opportunities.
- Attend university and college fairs, if they are offered in your area.
- Attend a **PREPSKILLS® SAT** and **US Admissions Information Seminar** (register at www.PREPSKILLS.com).

Grade 11

- In the fall, register for an SAT preparation course, PREPSKILLS® eight-week SAT program.
    - Consider how well you do on your diagnostic test, as well as the final mock SAT test that PREPSKILLS® offers its students. These will offer you a general indication of what your ultimate score on the SAT will be. Consider taking extra (or private) training sessions if you fall short of your college's required SAT/ACT score range.
- Identify five to ten of the colleges you would like to apply to, and start to familiarise yourself with their admissions websites.
- Register and write the SAT by the end of Grade 11, ideally right after you have completed your SAT preparation course. Remember to register for the SAT, approximately 2 months in advance of any particular test date, to ensure that there is a spot for you at the testing centre!
- **Register for, and write, your SAT Subject Tests by the end of Grade 11,** especially if your intention is to apply for early admission.
- Plan visits to colleges so you can determine whether the campus environment suits your needs and satisfies your hopes.

Early application deadlines and early action decisions

For early admissions, many colleges require SAT or ACT scores to be submitted by early November in your grade 12 year. Keep this in mind when developing your action plan for the year. Students can consult www.collegeboard.org for more information regarding the dates and registration deadlines associated with early decision applications.

https://bigfuture.collegeboard.org/get-in/applying-101/the-facts-about-applying-early-is-it-right-for-you

GRADE 12

- Review your list of chosen colleges. Go through the list with your school guidance counsellor to see whether he/she has any particular advice or knows students who have applied successfully in the past.
- Go online and download the application form(s) and financial aid information from each college on your list.

Make a master calendar that indicates the following items:

  - Test dates, fees, and deadlines.
  - College application due dates.
  - Financial aid applications and their respective deadlines.
  - Recommendations, transcripts, and other materials required for your applications.
  - Any deadlines that your own high school might stipulate for application materials, such as transcripts or financial aid packages, including graduation awards.

- Determine which people you want to ask to serve as your academic references and approach them regarding recommendation letters as soon as possible.
  - Give each person a copy of your curriculum vitae, transcript, and a list of any specific items you would like mentioned in the recommendation letter(s).
- Write draft copies of your application essays and ask teachers, parents, and friends to read, and offer critiques, your drafts.

DEADLINES

Note that most college applications are due between January 1st and February 15th. Check the college's website for deadlines.

DO keep copies of everything you submit.

DO have your high school send your transcript to your colleges directly.

DO contact the colleges you've applied to, (best done by telephone), in order to confirm they have received your application materials. Always take note of the contact person's name, and date as well as the time of your call. This way, if your application goes missing, you have proof that you submitted it on time.

ACCEPTANCE PROCEDURES

Just because you've received an acceptance letter does not mean your job is done.

Assuming you have the time to do so, you should visit the college campus that you are most interested in attending, before making your final decision. Sometimes a personal visit changes a person's opinion, entirely. Before rejecting one school in favour of another, get some personal experience.

Once you've decided where you'll be going to college, make sure to send in your acceptance letter with any requisite (non-refundable) deposits. These must reach the college by the stipulated deadline (usually by May 1st), to ensure your place is not given away to someone on a waiting list.

You must also send your rejections of offers from other colleges; not doing so indicates a lack of organization and poor professional behavior, on your part.

PUT ON A WAITING LIST?

All colleges will generate a wait-list of candidates, who may be allowed entry into the school, if some of the successful applicants did not accept their offers.

Each year, the number of wait-list candidates, that any college admits, will vary drastically. Wait-lists can range from 100 students (for small colleges) to 1000 students (for big colleges). The number of open admission spots will also vary on a yearly basis, depending on the school's budget, its staffing capacities and requirements, and any curricular reforms that may be instituted that year. Therefore, a school may or may not draw from its wait-list of candidates to fill its undergraduate ranks, in any given year.

If you find you have been put on a waiting list, make sure to contact the admissions office immediately, to let them know that you are still interested (if you are). Make sure to ask the admissions officers what you can do to strengthen your application. Many colleges will allow students to submit updates to their applications later in the year, in order to reassess whether they will be admitted.

ATHLETE'S WORLD

National Collegiate Athletic Association (NCAA)

If you're an athlete and you're looking to gain entry to an American college based on your sporting talents, one of the first stops you should make is the **National Collegiate Athletic Association (NCAA).**

This body is a voluntary organization, formed by American colleges and universities. It aims to bolster both the educational and athletic achievements of student-athletes.

The NCAA does not govern college sports per se. Rather, the colleges and universities that are members of the organization appoint and elect representatives who sit on various committees, which carry out governing duties. Those committees govern college-level athletics according to the interests of the college and university members. Thus, the NCAA calls itself a "bottom up" organization.

The NCAA champions a specific academic and athletic mandate, which aims to ensure fair, safe, equitable, and sportsmanlike behaviour in college sports. It aims to integrate intercollegiate athletics into higher education so sports can form an integral part of the student's experience. One of the ways in which the NCAA does this is by helping athletes, around the world, gain entry to American colleges, with funding to support their studies (either in the form of sports scholarships or bursary support).

NCAA-sponsored sports

Fall Sports
Cross Country (M)
Cross Country (W)
Field Hockey (W)
Football (M)
Soccer (M)
Soccer (W)
Volleyball (W)
Water Polo (M)

Spring Sports
Baseball (M)
Golf (M)
Golf (W)
Lacrosse (M)
Lacrosse (W)
Outdoor Track and Field (M)
Outdoor Track and Field (W)
Rowing (W)
Softball (W)
Tennis (M)
Tennis (W)
Volleyball (M)
Water Polo (W)

Winter Sports
Basketball (M)
Basketball (W)
Bowling (W)
Fencing (M)
Fencing (W)
Gymnastics (M)
Gymnastics (W)
Ice Hockey (M)
Ice Hockey (W)
Indoor Track and Field (M)
Indoor Track and Field (W)
Rifle (M)
Rifle (W)
Skiing (M)
Skiing (W)
Swimming and Diving (M)
Swimming and Diving (W)
Wrestling (M)

Emerging Sports
Equestrian (W)
Rugby (W)
Sand Volleyball (W)
Triathlon (W)

DEMYSTIFYING THE NCAA

The NCAA was established in 1906. Currently, it serves as the overarching governing body for more than 1,200 colleges, universities, conferences, and organizations. Member colleges (and their representatives) develop rules and regulations that govern athletic eligibility and athletic competitions, for each of the three NCAA divisions.

NCAA membership includes:

- 350 active Division I members
- 307 active Division II members
- 450 active Division III members

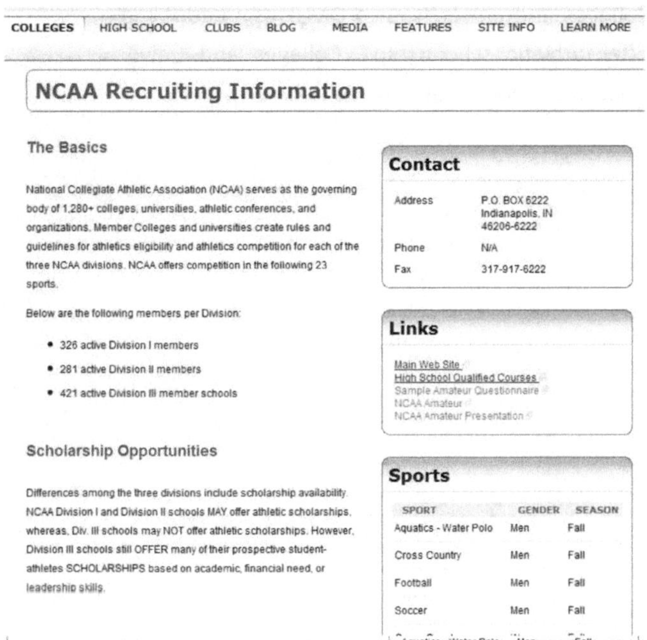

For specific information related to the academic requirements, for student athletes, you must consult the NCAA's Resource Centre.

"The overwhelming majority of student-athletes will never earn a dime as a professional athlete. That's why the terms 'student' and 'athlete' are synonymous within the NCAA: When the athlete can no longer play, the student can still succeed."

www.ncaa.org

Colleges and universities in Divisions I and II may offer athletic scholarships. Colleges and universities in Division III, usually, do not.

Eligibility Centre Contact Information

NCAA Eligibility Centre
Certification Processing
P.O. Box 7136
Indianapolis, IN 46207-7136

Package or overnight delivery:
1802 Alonzo Watford Sr. Drive
Indianapolis, IN 46202

Web address:
www.ncaaclearinghouse.net
www.eligibilitycenter.org

Eligibility Centre customer service representatives
8 a.m. to 6 p.m.,
Eastern time, Monday through Friday.
U.S. callers (toll free): 877/262-1492
International callers: 317/917-6222
Fax: 317/968-5100

When to call the NCAA?
The NCAA recommends you call their offices directly if your available resources are unable to answer all your questions about topics, such as:

- *What are the rules and regulations related to initial eligibility?*
- *What are the rules and regulations related to amateurism?*
- *What are the regulations about transferring from one college to another?*
- *What are the rules about athletic scholarships and how can they be reduced or cancelled?*
- *I have an education-impacting disability. Are there any other requirements for me?*

NCAA
P.O. Box 7110
Indianapolis, IN 46207
Phone: 317-917-6222

NCAA Eligibility Centre

Students who are hoping to compete, in the NCAA, must register with the Eligibility Centre. Note that the NCAA Clearing House is used to certify the amateur status of each athlete as part of the NCAA Eligibility Centre.

The NCAA Eligibility Centre will certify the academic, and amateur credentials, of all college-bound student-athletes who wish to compete in NCAA Division I or II athletics.

The Eligibility Centre manages student's applications for athletic eligibility. It also processes their initial certifications, although the certification process is one that is carried out in collaboration with the colleges, to which each student applies. More information about the Eligibility Centre, and its certification process, can be located in the *Guide for the College-Bound Student-Athletes,* an online guidebook published by the NCAA. The *Guide* is available on the Eligibility Centre web site.

www.eligibilitycenter.org

ncaa.org

The NCAA Eligibility Centre has developed a user-friendly website, geared towards prospective student-athletes. The information and resources are broken down clearly, with interactive features for parents and high school students. Along with jumpforward.com, this makes for a great resource for all student-athletes.

Once you find your way to the Eligibility Centre website, imaged on the previous page, click on the link for NCAA College-Bound Student-Athletes.

The link below will take you to the following site:

http://web3.ncaa.org/ECWR2/NCAA_EMS/NCAA_EMS.html

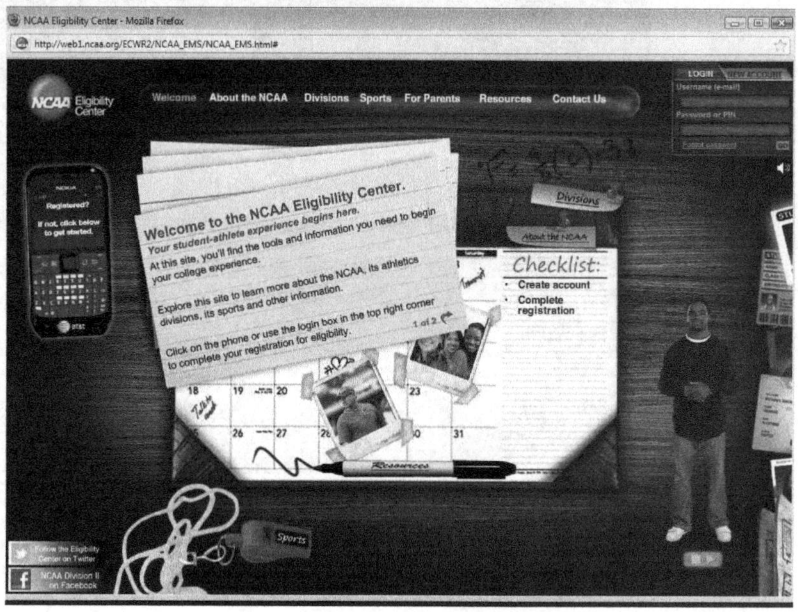

Here, you can locate information related specifically to applications made by International (i.e. Canadian) student-athletes.

Before you apply for the Eligibility Centre, it's best to go through the following check list:

- ☐ **Valid Email Address**. You need a valid email address that you check regularly for any possible updates that the NCAA Eligibility Center might send. If you do not currently have one, there are several providers who provide free accounts (e.g., AOL, Gmail, Hotmail, Yahoo, etc.).

- ☐ **Basic Personal Information**. This includes information such as your name, gender, date of birth, contact information and a list of any other countries in which you have lived.

- ☐ **Basic Education History**. This includes a list of all high schools or secondary schools you have attended and the dates during which you attended them.

- ☐ **Additional Coursework**. This includes details pertaining to any coursework you may have taken in addition to your normal high school or secondary school education (e.g., courses taken to improve a grade, summer school courses taken at a location other than your high school or secondary school, courses taken at a college or junior college, or any type of correspondence or internet courses).

- ☐ **Sports Participation History**. This includes details for any teams with which you have practiced or played or certain events in which you may have participated, as well as information about any individuals that have advised you or marketed your skills in a particular sport

- ☐ **Payment**. The registration fee is $75 for U.S., U.S. Territories and Canadian students (U.S. Territories include American Samoa, Guam, Northern Mariana Islands, Puerto Rico and U.S. Virgin Islands); and $130 for all other international students. The NCAA Eligibility Center accepts Visa, MasterCard, Discover and American Express. If you are a U.S. resident, you can choose to pay by electronic check. Some individuals *may* qualify to apply for a fee waiver.

Adapted from:
http://fs.ncaa.org/Docs/eligibility_center/Student_Resources/Registration_Checklist.pdf

Now that you have gone through the check list on the previous page, it's time to register. A summary of the registration guidelines is as follows:

Information for International Student-Athletes

What is the NCAA Eligibility Centre?

The eligibility centre is an agency which will provide initial-eligibility certification for all prospective student-athletes wishing to compete as freshman at NCAA member institutions offering Division I or II athletics. The eligibility centre is not a placement agency or an admissions office - it will not locate a college/institution for student-athletes to attend. The eligibility centre will provide the student's initial-eligibility certification results to all colleges/universities that request to receive this information.

Who must register with the eligibility centre? Any prospective student-athlete who will enrol in college as a freshman and plans to compete in NCAA Division I or Division II athletics must register with the eligibility centre.

How do I register with the eligibility centre?

There are several documents required to apply to the eligibility centre. International student-athletes must submit all of the following items:

1. Fill out the eligibility centre online application for International Student-Athletes.

2. Proof of graduation in the form of a final diploma, leaving exam, maturity certificate, record of learning, higher certificate, or another document that shows completion of upper secondary or pre-university schooling must be submitted to the eligibility centre.

3. Original academic records [or certified (attested) copies of the original documents] and certified, literal English translations for records not originally in English sent (not faxed) to the eligibility centre.

4. Score(s) from either the ACT or SAT standardized tests, reported directly to the eligibility centre by requesting code "9999."

5. Ensure that if you need an F1 student visa, you meet the specific requirements for admissions eligibility, financial ability, and academic status.

After you graduate

If your eligibility status is requested by a member institution, the eligibility centre will review your final transcript and proof of graduation to make a final certification decision according to NCAA standards. **Note, however, if you fail to submit all the documents required or if no member institution requests your eligibility status, your incomplete file will be discarded after three years, requiring you to pay a new fee if certification is requested after that time.**

Adapted from http://www.ncaa.org/student-athletes/future/international-student-athletes

THE NEXT STEP

Making the decision to submit your applications to American Universities is a big step, but knowing what to do next is the critical part. How do you market your talent, and accomplishments, to American athletic programs that don't typically recruit heavily in Canada? The answer is the internet, via the resources at your disposal on jumpforward.com.

PREPSKILLS® strongly recommends any student-athletes looking to seriously compete for roster spots in American universities should utilize the free tools on jumpforward.com. The first step is to click on 'Get Your Recruiting Handbook' on the JumpForward home page. JumpForward's *Playbook* infuses information from the NCAA and other governing bodies, former NCAA coaches, athletes, athletic department employees, and other valuable sources, into a step-by-step process that works hand-in-hand with JumpForward's online tools.

Your next step, as outlined in *The Playbook*, is to create your JumpForward Sport Profile. The key to being recruited is to take a proactive role, and empower yourself. Take the time to make your Sport Profile the best possible example of your value, as a prospect for coaches.

You can register for your Sport Profile straight from the jumpforward.com home page. The Profile acts as your athletic resume, with any and all information that will showcase yourself to 50,000 college coaches.

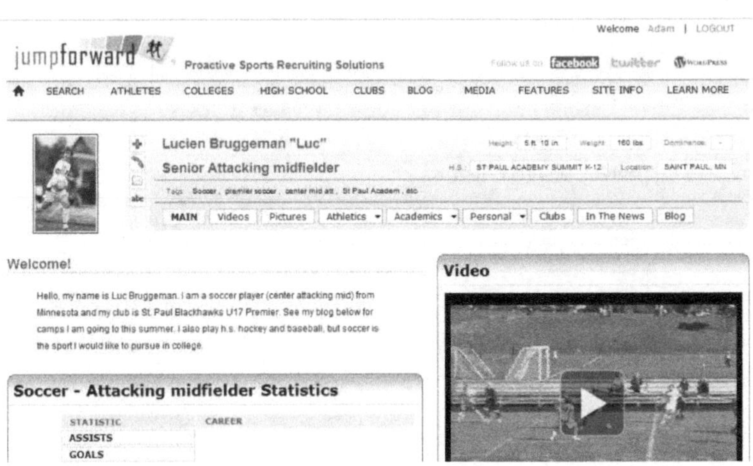

It is important to fill out the profile completely, to paint a picture of who you are. Coaches and administrators like well-rounded prospects. This includes your athletic and academic information, pictures, highlight videos, links to news articles, and any other special information about you!

Communication and Connection

Now that you have your Sport Profile page filled in to showcase yourself, the next step is to research the schools you want to attend and connect with the coaches. JumpForward has the tools for this step. Starting with the **College Search Database**, you are able to search for schools, find the contact information for 50,000 coaches, and connect directly with the 'Click to Call' technology. Don't know what to say? JumpForward has a complete FAQ and notes section, for you to keep track of your calls, as well as email templates.

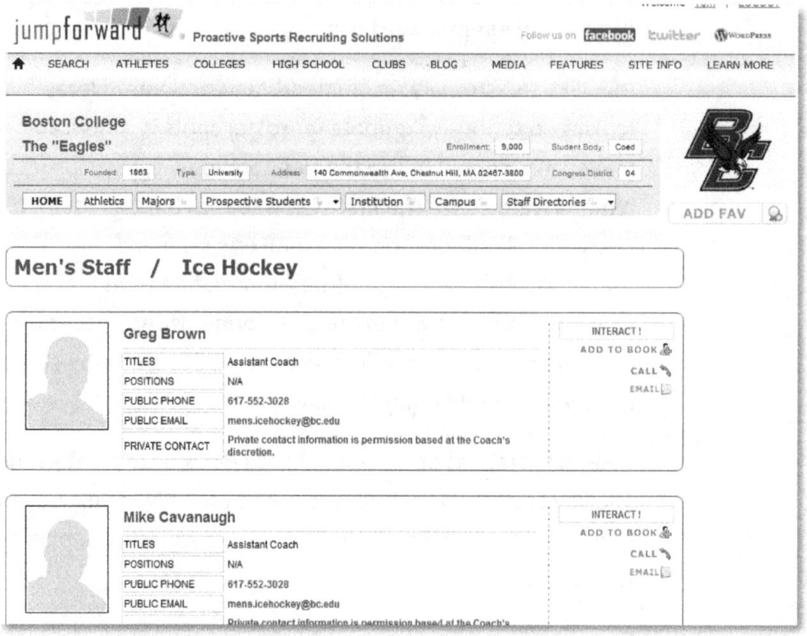

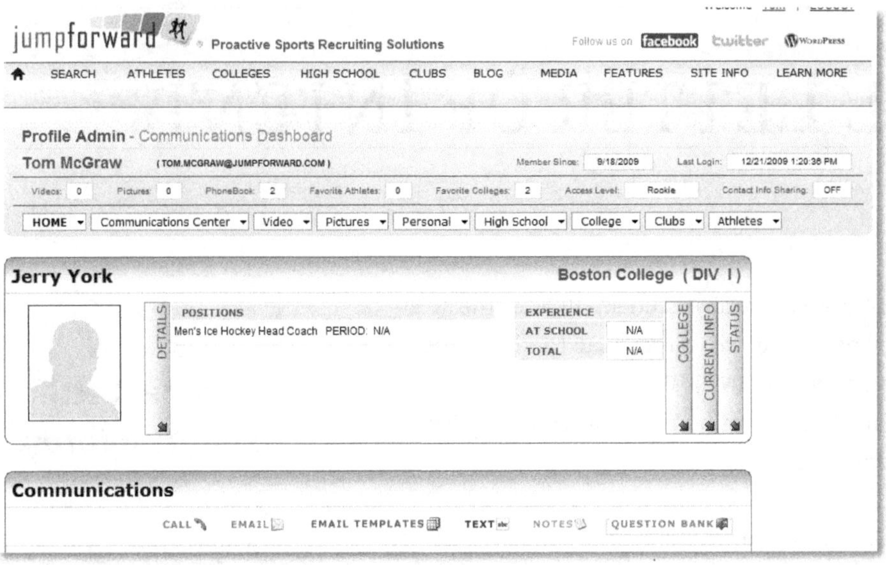

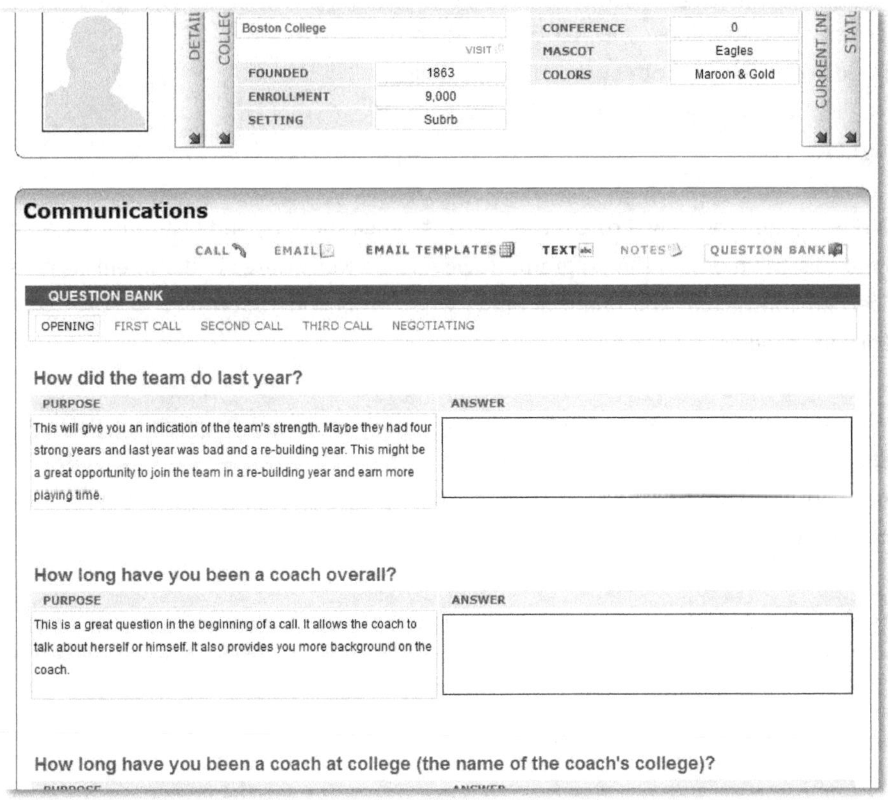

Communication Center

After finding the coach you want to contact in the College Search Database, click 'Add to Book'. This will add them to your contacts book so you can begin making a connection.

Now you can call, email (with your own words or templates), take notes, and use the FAQs to guide conversation and ask the right questions.

NATIONAL LETTER OF INTENT (NLI)

If you're a prospective student-athlete, the NCAA Eligibility Centre will direct you to the **National Letter of Intent (NLI)** site, as part of your application for certification as a Division I or Division II student-athlete.

The NLI was started in 1964. At the time, it included seven conferences and eight independent institutions. Today, the program includes 650 Division I and Division II institutions. The NLI organization is governed and managed both by the NCAA Eligibility Centre and the Collegiate Commissioners Association (CCA).

National Letter of Intent contact information

Website
www.nationalletter.org

Telephone
1-877-262-1492

The NLI is a voluntary body. Prospective students, their parents, and institutions are not required to sign up or join the program. However, the NLI ensures that student-athletes gain certain contractual and financial rights when embarking upon their college-based athletic, and academic, careers.

The NLI website, for instance, indicates that a student agrees to attend a particular college or university for at least one year. It obligates the student to fulfil this commitment and it obligates other colleges to stop attempting to recruit that student during the, contractual, one-year period.

www.nationalletter.org

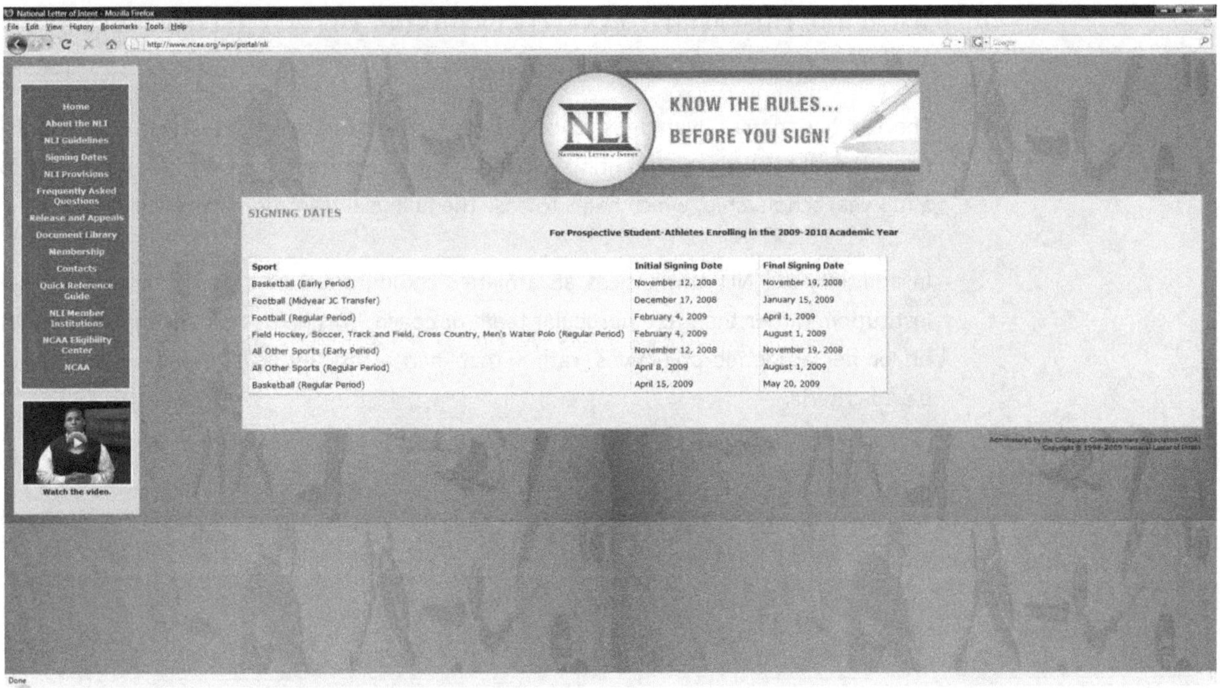
KNOW THE RULES...
BEFORE YOU SIGN!

SIGNING DATES

For Prospective Student-Athletes Enrolling in the 2009-2010 Academic Year

Sport	Initial Signing Date	Final Signing Date
Basketball (Early Period)	November 12, 2008	November 19, 2008
Football (Midyear JC Transfer)	December 17, 2008	January 15, 2009
Football (Regular Period)	February 4, 2009	April 1, 2009
Field Hockey, Soccer, Track and Field, Cross Country, Men's Water Polo (Regular Period)	February 4, 2009	August 1, 2009
All Other Sports (Early Period)	November 12, 2008	November 19, 2008
All Other Sports (Regular Period)	April 8, 2009	August 1, 2009
Basketball (Regular Period)	April 15, 2009	May 20, 2009

Why sign the National Letter of Intent?

The NLI website states:

By signing a National Letter of Intent, a prospective student-athlete agrees to attend the designated college or university for one academic year.

Pursuant to the terms of the National Letter of Intent program, participating institutions agree to provide athletics financial aid, for one academic year, to the student-athlete, provided he/she is admitted to the institution and is eligible for financial aid under NCAA rules.

An important provision of the National Letter of Intent program is a recruiting prohibition applied after a prospective student-athlete signs a Letter of Intent. This prohibition requires participating institutions to cease recruitment of a prospective student-athlete once a National Letter of Intent is signed with another institution.

What are the specific benefits of joining the National Letter of Intent?

The NLI has many advantages to both prospective student-athletes and participating educational institutions. The primary benefit is it guarantees student-athletes access to a full-year scholarship, which helps to ease the financial transition into college life.

In addition, the NLI emphasizes an athlete's commitment to a particular educational institution, rather than to a particular team or coach. This helps to focus the student on his or her academic objectives, rather than narrowing the college choices to sports-based criteria.

Academic Eligibility Requirements: Division I

Note the following requirements are set within the context of American high school curricula.

The NCAA can provide Canadian students with equivalency measures. Make sure to contact the NCAA early on to obtain a list of equivalent requirements for Canadians.

If you want to participate in athletics, or receive an athletic scholarship in your first year of college life, you must ensure you obtain the following qualifications:

Full Qualifiers, Academic Redshirts, and Nonqualifiers

- **Division I Full Qualifiers**
  Being a Full Qualifier entitles you to:
  - Practice and compete for your college during your first year of college
  - Receive an athletic scholarship during your first year of college

- **Division I Academic Redshirt**
  As an Academic Redshirt, you will:
  - Be entitled to practice for your college during your first year of college
  - Not be able to compete for your college during your first year of college
  - Be entitled to receive an athletic scholarship during your first year of college

- **Division I Nonqualifier**
  As a Nonqualifier, you will:
  - Not be able to practice for your college during your first year of college
  - Not be able to compete for your college during your first year of college
  - Not be able to receive athletic scholarships during your first year of college

ELIGIBILITY REQUIREMENTS: DIVISION I

You must successfully graduate from high school.
You must complete the following 16 core courses (from Grade 9 to Grade 12) at the normal academic level:

- four years of English
- three years of math (algebra 1 or higher)
- two years of natural/physical science (including one year of laboratory science if it is offered by your high school)
- one extra year of English, math, or natural/physical science
- two years of social science
- four years of extra core courses (including foreign languages, non-doctrinal religious studies, or philosophy)

You must earn the minimum required grade-point average (GPA) in your core courses.

You must achieve a combined SAT or ACT sum score that matches your core-course grade-point average, and test score sliding scale (e.g., a 2.400 core-course grade-point average needs an 860 SAT). See the **Sliding Scale Table** on the next page.

SLIDING GPA SCALE FOR DIVISION I ELIGIBILITY

	DIVISION I FULL QUALIFER SLIDING SCALE		
	Core GPA	SAT Reading/Math	ACT Sum
	3.550	400	37
	3.525	410	38
	3.500	420	39
	3.475	430	40
	3.450	440	41
	3.425	450	41
	3.400	460	42
	3.375	470	42
	3.350	480	43
	3.325	490	44
	3.300	500	44
	3.275	510	45
	3.250	520	46
	3.225	530	46
	3.200	540	47
	3.175	550	47
	3.150	560	48
	3.125	570	49
	3.100	580	49
	3.075	590	50
	3.050	600	50
	3.025	610	51
	3.000	620	52
	2.975	630	52
	2.950	640	53
	2.925	650	53
	2.900	660	54
	2.875	670	55
	2.850	680	56
	2.825	690	56
	2.800	700	57
	2.775	710	58
	2.750	720	59
	2.725	730	60
	2.700	740	61
	2.675	750	61
	2.650	760	62
	2.625	770	63
	2.600	780	64
	2.575	790	65
	2.550	800	66
	2.525	810	67
	2.500	820	68
	2.475	830	69

Canadian Prospective Student-Athletes

Core-course listings for each province are now listed on the eligibility centre website under the following high school codes:

Quebec	998001
Saskatchewan	998002
Ontario	998003
Alberta	998004
British Columbia	998005
Manitoba	998006
Newfoundland and Labrador	998007
Prince Edward Island	998008
Nova Scotia	998009
New Brunswick	998010
Yukon Territory	998011
Northwest Territory	998012
Nunavut	998013

	2.450	840	70
	2.425	850	70
	2.400	860	71
	2.375	870	72
	2.350	880	73
	2.325	890	74
	2.300	900	75
ACADEMIC REDSHIRT	2.299	910	76
	2.275	910	76
	2.250	920	77
	2.225	930	78
	2.200	940	79
	2.175	950	80
	2.150	960	81
	2.125	970	82
	2.100	980	83
	2.075	990	84
	2.050	1000	85
	2.025	1010	86
	2.000	1020	86

Requirement to Graduate with Your High School Class

In order to qualify for entrance as a student-athlete, students must ensure they graduate with their Grade 9 cohort.

In other words, if you require an extra year of upgrading in order to complete your high school diploma studies, you will not qualify as a Division I student-athlete, with the NCAA.

If you graduate from high school in eight semesters with your class, you may use one core course completed in the year after graduation (summer or academic year) to meet NCAA Division I eligibility requirements. You may complete the core course at a location other than the high school from which you graduated, and you may initially enrol full time at a collegiate institution, at any time after the completion of the core course.

ELIGIBILITY REQUIREMENTS: DIVISION II (2016)

If you want to enrol in a Division II college, and you want to participate in athletics or receive an athletic scholarship in your first year of college life, you must ensure you obtain the following qualifications:

Full Qualifiers, Partial Qualifiers, and Nonqualifiers

- **Division II Full Qualifiers**
  Being a Full Qualifier entitles you to:
  - Practice and compete for your college during your first year of college
  - Receive an athletic scholarship during your first year of college

- **Division II Partial Qualifier**
  As a Partial Qualifier, you will:
  - Be entitled to practice for your college during your first academic term
  - Not be able to compete for your college during your first year of college
  - Be entitled to receive an athletic scholarship during your first year of college

- **Division I Nonqualifier**
  As a Nonqualifier, you will:
  - Not be able to practice for your college during your first year of college
  - Not be able to compete for your college during your first year of college
  - Not be able to receive athletic scholarships during your first year of college

ELIGIBILITY REQUIREMENTS: DIVISION II

You must graduate from high school
You must complete the following 16 core courses:

- *three years of English;*
- *two years of math (algebra 1 or higher)*
- *two years of natural/physical science (including one year of laboratory science if it is offered by your high school)*
- *three additional years of English, math, or natural/physical science*
- *two years of social science*
- *four years of extra core courses (including foreign languages, non-doctrinal religious studies, or philosophy)*
- *earn a 2.00 grade-point average, or better, in your core courses*
- *earn a combined SAT score of 820 or an ACT sum score of 68*

IMPORTANT!

The NCAA reminds students that the Eligibility Centre academic rules do not guarantee admission into a college.

The academic requirements outlined on previous pages are for the NCAA's purposes only.

You must apply for general admission with your college of choice directly. In doing so, you must follow all the standard admission procedures outlined in the earlier sections of this manual!

NCAA Course Requirements		
Course Area	**Division I**	**Division II**
English	4	3
Mathamatics (Algebra 1 or higher level)	3	2
Natural or Physical Science	2	2
Additional English, Math, or Science	1	3
Social Science	2	2
Additional Courses (foreign language, nondoctrinal religion or philosophy)	4	4
Total	16	16

NCAA Testing Requirements	
Core-Course Average GPA (2.00 to 4.00) DIV II Minimum Testing Requirements	
ACT	68
SAT	820

The Knowledge Center

All the academic and amateurism requirements laid out in this section are also laid out clearly on jumpforward.com. In fact, if you are finding all these requirements to be a bit overwhelming, JumpForward has built an **NCAA Core Course Tracking Worksheet** you can use to track your progress.

The Worksheet mirrors the piece of paper the NCAA hands out to prospective student-athletes. Inputting your grades each semester allows you to see what you have accomplished, what is left to reach, and what your required standardized tests scores are.

No guessing. No calculations. JumpForward does the work for you!

Grade Tracking Worksheet

This page gives you examples of information available as part of your JumpForward Profile. Simply sign in and you'll find the NCAA Worksheet under the 'High School' tab of your profile home page, among other features.

NCAA Course Tracking Worksheet

PRIVACY

Freshmen

CORE COURSE & DESCRIPTION			PERIOD	CREDIT	GRADE	GPA
Mathematics	Geometry	×	1st Semester	0.50	C	2
English	Weeding	×	2nd Semester	0.50	C+	2
	Freshmen Year Totals - Credits & GPA :			1		2.00

Sophomore

CORE COURSE & DESCRIPTION			PERIOD	CREDIT	GRADE	GPA
Social Science	Trimming	×	1st Semester	0.50	C	2
Foreign Language	Judism	×	1st Semester	0.50	A-	4
Philosophy	French Impressionism	×	1st Semester	0.50	B	3
Foreign Language	Cleaning	×	2nd Semester	0.50	C-	2
	Sophomore Year Totals - Credits & GPA :			2		2.75

Junior

CORE COURSE & DESCRIPTION			PERIOD	CREDIT	GRADE	GPA
Natural Science	Edging	×	2nd Semester	0.50	B+	3
Physical Science	Mowing	×	2nd Semester	0.50	A	4
	Junior Year Totals - Credits & GPA :			1		3.50

Senior

CORE COURSE & DESCRIPTION			PERIOD	CREDIT	GRADE	GPA
Mathematics	Cooking	×	1st Semester	0.50	A-	4
Foreign Language	British	×	1st Semester	0.50	F	0
Natural Science	Mopping	×	2nd Semester	0.50	B+	3
Philosophy	Vacuming	×	2nd Semester	0.50	C-	2
	Senior Year Totals - Credits & GPA :			2		2.25

Worksheet Totals & Minimum Test Scores

PRIVACY

TOTAL CREDITS	OVERALL GPA	MINIMUM ACT SCORE	MINIMUM SAT SCORE
6	2.58	65	790

NCAA Eligible Courses – Ontario Course Codes

English	
Canadian Literature	EAT3M
Canadian Literature	ETC3M
English 10	ENG2D/EAE2D
English 11	ENG3U/EAE3U
English 12	ENG4U/EAE4U
English 9	ENG1D/EAE1D
English Literature	EAL4U
English: Contemp Aboriginal Voices	NBE3U
French 10 (Native Language)	FRA2D
French 11 (Native Language)	FRA3U
French 12 (Native Language)	FRA4U
French 9 (Native Language)	FRA1D
Studies In Literature	ETS4U
The Writer's Craft	EWC4U
Mathematics	
Adv Functions & Intro Calculus	MCB4U
Advanced Functions	MHF4U
Calculus & Vectors	MCV4U
Functions & Relations	MCR3U
Functions	MCF3M
Geometry & Discrete Math	MGA4U
Mathematics & Data Management	MDM4U
Principles Of Math 10	MPM2D
Principles Of Math 9	MPM1D
Natural/Physical Science	
Biology	SBI3U
Biology	SBI4U
Chemistry	SCH3U
Chemistry	SCH4U
Earth & Space Science	SES4U
Environmental Science	SVN3M
Physics	SPH3U
Physics	SPH4U

Natural/Physical Science	
Science 10	SNC2D
Science 11	SNC3M
Science 12	SNC4M
Science 9	SNC1D
Social Science	
Aboriginal Governance	NDG4M
American History	CHA3U
Analyzing Current Econ Issues	CIA4U
Canada: Hist, Identity, Culture	CHI4U
Canadian & Int'L Law	CLN4U
Canadian & World Politics	CPW4U
Canadian And World Issues	CGW4U
Canadian History 20Th Century	CHC2D
Challenge & Change In Society	HSB4M
Challenge & Change In Society	HSB4U
Civics	CHV2O
Classical Civilization	LVV4U
Current Aboriginal Issues	NDA3M
Environ & Resource Management	CGR4M
Equity And Social Justice	HSE4M
Families In Canada	HHS4U
Gender Studies	HSG3M
Geography Of Canada	CGC1D
Geography Patterns & Issues	CGD3M
Geomatics	CGO4M
Ind & Families In A Div Society	HHS4M
International Business	BBB4M
Intro To Anthro, Psych & Soc	HSP3M
Intro To Anthro, Psych & Soc	HSP3U
Issues Of Indigenous Peoples	NDW4M
Physical Geography	CGF3M
The Individual & The Economy	CIE3M
Understanding Canadian Law	CLU3M

Social Science	
World Cultures	HSC4M
World Geog: Human Patterns	CGU4U
World Hist: The West & The World	CHY4U
World History 16Th Century	CHW3M
Additional Core Courses	
Cantonese 1	LKDAD
Cantonese 2	LKDBD
Core French 1	FSF1D
Core French 2	FSF2D
Core French 3	FSF3U
Core French 4	FSF4U
Croatian	LBCCU
Extended French 1	FEF1D
Extended French 2	FEF2D
Extended French 3	FEF3U
Extended French 4	FEF4U
Farsi	LYGDU
French Immersion 1	FIF1D
French Immersion 2	FIF2D
French Immersion 3	FIF3U
French Immersion 4	FIF4U
German 1	LWGAD
German 2	LWGBD
German 3	LWGCU
German 4	LWGDU
Greek 1	LBGAD
Greek 1	LVGAD
Greek 2	LBGBD
Greek 2	LVGBU
Greek 3	LBGCU
Greek 3	LVGCU
Greek 4	LBGDU
Hebrew 1	LYHAD
Hebrew 11	LYHCU
Hebrew 2	LYHBD
Italian 1	LWIAD
Italian 2	LWIBD
Italian 3	LWICU
Italian 4	LWIDU

Additional Core Courses	
Japanese 10	LKJBD
Japanese 11	LKJCU
Japanese 12	LKJDU
Japanese 9	LKJAD
Latin 1	LVLAD
Latin 2	LVLBU
Latin 3	LVLCU
Lithuanian 10	LLUBD
Lithuanian 11	LLUCU
Lithuanian 12	LLUDU
Lithuanian 9	LLUAD
Mandarin 10	LKMBD
Mandarin 11	LKMCU
Mandarin 12	LKMDU
Mandarin 9	LKMAD
Philosophy	HZT4U
Philosophy: The Big Questions	HZB3M
Polish 10	LRPBD
Polish 11	LRPCU
Polish 12	LRPDU
Polish 9	LRQAD
Portuguese 10	LWPBD
Portuguese 11	LWPCU
Religious Education	HRE4M
Russian 10	LRZBD
Russian 11	LRZCU
Russian 12	LRZDU
Spanish 10	LWS2D
Spanish 10	LWSBD
Spanish 11	LWSCU
Spanish 12	LWSDU
Spanish 9	LWS1D
Spanish 9	LWSAD
Ukrainian 10	LRUBD
Ukrainian 11	LRUCU
Ukrainian 12	LRUDU
Vietnamese 10	LPVBD1
World Religions	HRT3M

SUMMARY OF NCAA ELIGIBILITY RULES

When should a student register with the NCAA Eligibility Centre?

Students should register with the Eligibility Centre at the beginning of their junior year in high school (Grade 11). Using JumpForward's tools to track your progress can begin freshman year (Grade 9).

At the end of the student's junior year, a transcript, which includes six semesters of grades, should be sent to the Eligibility Centre from the high school.

Students should also have their SAT or ACT scores forwarded directly to the Eligibility Centre (use the code "9999" whenever you take the exam).

COMMON QUESTIONS

What requirements do I need to be able to practice, play, and get a scholarship at an NCAA Division I or II college or university?

You need to complete the following:
1. Graduate from high school.
2. Complete a minimum of 16 core courses for Divisions I and II.
3. Present the required grade-point average (GPA) (see the **Sliding Scale for Student-Athletes** for Division I, or a Grade Point Average of 2.000 for Division II).
4. Present a qualifying test score on either the SAT or ACT (for Division I, see the **Sliding Scale** on the previous page; for Division II, a minimum SAT score requirement of 820 or an ACT sum score of 68 is required).
5. Complete the amateurism questionnaire and request final amateurism certification.

How do I know whether the courses I am taking will count as core courses?

You need to look at your high school's NCAA List of Approved Core Courses. Follow these steps:

1. Stays the same as what it was already
2. Click on "NCAA College-Bound Student-Athletes"
3. Click on "Resources"
4. Click on "List of NCAA Courses"
5. Input your high school's CEEB code or search by your province using these codes: (list the content from the side-bar of page 139)
6. Review the list.

Important*: If a core course you took is not on the list, it will not be used in your eligibility determination. Courses that appear on your transcript must match what's on the list.*

For more information and for Frequently Asked Questions about NCAA Eligibility, view the following website:

www.ncaa.org/about/frequently-asked-questions-about-ncaa

Eligibility Requirements: Division III

Division III

Division III does not use the Eligibility Centre.

Contact your Division III college or university to inquire about its specific policies on admission, financial aid, practice, and competition.

Adapted from the 2008-09 Guide for the College-Bound Student Athletes: Follow the path to success—as a student athlete, published by the NCAA Eligibility Centre (2009).

Ontario Hockey League (OHL)

What is the OHL?

The OHL originated with the Ontario Hockey Association (OHA), which was first formed in 1890. The OHA encompassed junior ice hockey in Ontario for over a century. In 1933, the organization's junior division was divided into Junior A and Junior B. In 1972, the junior A level was further divided into Tier I (Major Junior A) and Tier II (Minor Junior A). In 1974, the first tier, "Major Junior A," became the Ontario Major Junior Hockey League (OMJHL) and began to operate independently of the OHA. In 1980, that organization officially became the **Ontario Hockey League (OHL)**.

At the time it separated from the OHA, the OHL gained complete control over its finances and ticket sales. Over the past three decades, the organization has gained increased media coverage and has become more widely popularized and broadcasted.

In the 1990s, the League expanded to include some American teams. There are currently 20 teams in the OHL, of which 17 are based in Ontario, two are based in Michigan, and one is based in Pennsylvania. The OHL is considered one route to a professional hockey career, running parallel to the NCAA recruitment process.

www.ontariohockeyleague.com

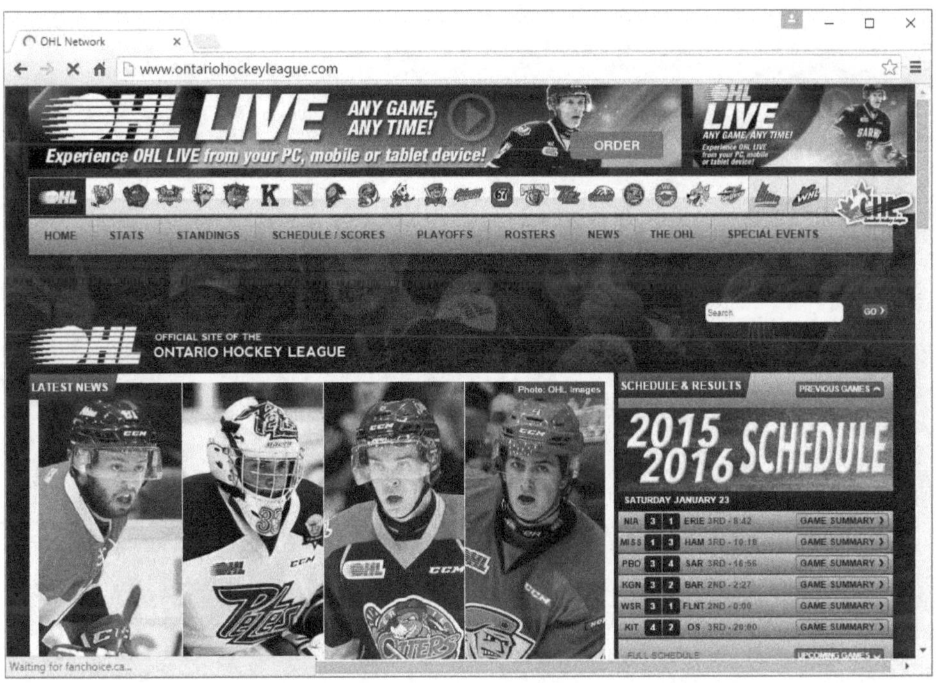

Academic Policy of the OHL

The OHL supports student-athletes by setting particular academic standards and educational goals for players within its league.

For example, the OHL expects that each of its teams will have an Educational Consultant to support the academic expectations, as outlined in the organization's Education Policy.

The OHL will:

- Convene seminars on a regular basis to inform parents of the opportunities available in the League.
- Convene meetings of the Education Consultants to plan and implement the educational initiatives of the League and of each team.
- Provide educational support material for all teams, players, and families, e.g., Making Your Mark in the OHL, Best of Both Worlds and OHL Education Manual.

Regarding the teams in the league, the OHL expects that:

- All teams will incur all educational costs of players, including tuition, books, and room and board, while playing for their OHL team.
- An Education Consultant will be available for all players and families.
- All educational needs will be addressed promptly. Strategies developed to ensure academic success for all players will be made available.
- Computer access will be provided for all players.
- Practice time will be scheduled around regular school days and hours.
- All players will be offered the opportunity to complete their academic program in the locale of the team when the season finishes.
- Regular communication occurs between the Education Consultant and Team Management.

Regarding players, the OHL expects that:

- All players adhere to their respective teams' Education Policy.
- All players attend high school until graduation.
- All players that enrol in educational programs are expected to participate fully in all classes and strive to maintain a passing grade.
- All players are encouraged to pursue post-secondary pathways.

The OHL education consultant is expected to do the following:

- Liaise with players, schools, teams, and parents.
- Communicate with Team Management to support the team's Education Policy.
- Facilitate the registration process with players in high school so they can pursue post-secondary academics.
- Provide academic counselling and support, including facilitating tutorial assistance when necessary.
- Support the League's educational initiatives.

OHL Scholarships

At the conclusion of a player's junior eligibility, the player has 18 months to access the OHL scholarship, thereby allowing the student to play minor professional hockey. While playing in the OHL, every player benefits from a full scholarship that covers tuition, compulsory fees, textbooks, and room and board (all costs are paid for by the OHL Member Team).

Once a player graduates from the OHL, that player will receive a minimum scholarship that pays for tuition, textbooks, and compulsory fees towards an undergraduate degree, for each year played in the Ontario Hockey League. The OHL Scholarship can be applied to university programs or diploma programs, including technical, trade, fire fighting, or emergency medical services diplomas.

OHL Academic Awards

Bobby Smith Trophy

The Bobby Smith Trophy is awarded annually to the OHL Scholastic Player of the Year who best combines high standards of play and academic excellence. The trophy is in honour of Bobby Smith, the former Ottawa 67's star who exhibited a high standard of excellence in his career. Each team's nominee for the award becomes a member of the OHL Scholastic Team of the Year.

The Roger Neilson Memorial Award

The Roger Neilson Memorial Award has been created to recognize the OHL's top academic player attending university. While coaching the Peterborough Petes in the late 1960's and early 1970's, Neilson was a pioneer in stressing the importance of education to all of his players. A former high school teacher, Neilson went on to a successful coaching career in the National Hockey League, and was inducted into the Hockey Hall of Fame in 2002. Neilson, a graduate of McMaster University in Hamilton, was also honoured with the Order of Canada in 2002. He passed away on June 21, 2003, after a long fight with cancer.

Ivan Tennant Memorial Award

The Ivan Tennant Memorial Award is presented annually to the OHL's Top Academic High School Player. Tennant, a former senior hockey player and Jr. B coach, spent a lifetime combining hockey and education. He was the Kitchener Rangers' Education Consultant for 20 years, and a key figure on the OHL's Education Consultants Committee. Tennant was instrumental in developing high education standards for the Rangers and the entire Ontario Hockey League, before he passed away on May 4, 2004.

Canadian Hockey League (CHL)

In addition to the Ontario Hockey League (OHL), a number of other leagues fall under the broad grouping headed by the **Canadian Hockey League (CHL),** they include the Western Hockey League and the Quebec Major Junior Hockey League. Each league offers its own respective scholarship program.

The Western Hockey League

The Western Hockey League started with just seven teams, based in the provinces of Saskatchewan and Alberta, in 1966. The WHL now has representation in all four Western Canadian provinces and the U.S. states of Oregon and Washington. With the addition of the Edmonton Oil Kings for the 2007-08 season, the WHL now consists of 22 member teams with 17 teams based in Canadian markets and 5 in the U.S. Pacific Northwest.

www.whl.ca

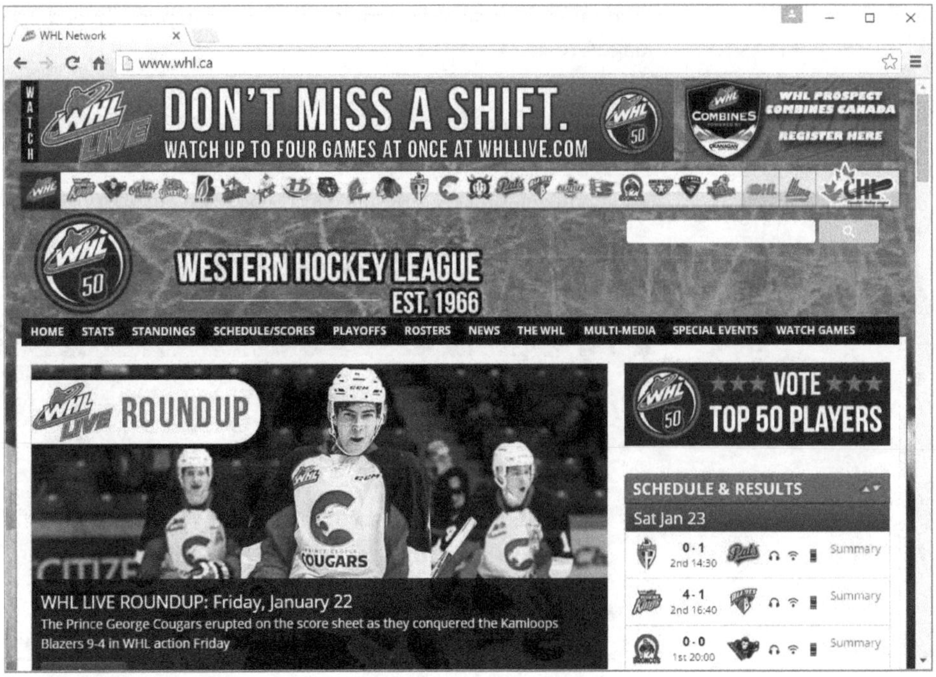

WHL Scholarships

For every season a player plays in the WHL, a player receives a full-year guaranteed scholarship, including tuition, textbooks, and compulsory fees, for any post-secondary institution of their choice. Players graduating from a four-year WHL career are eligible to receive four years of scholarship funding.

The WHL Scholarship, combined with additional financial assistance from universities in western Canada, make the WHL-Western Canadian Universities joint scholarship equivalent to any other offer available in North America today. The WHL is the leading provider of hockey scholarships in Western Canada. Each year, more than 230 WHL graduates receive a WHL Scholarship.

Quebec Major Junior Hockey League

The QMJHL includes 18 teams throughout Québec, the Atlantic Provinces, and New England. Its membership includes more than four hundred players aged 16 to 21 years old. These teens, and young adults, play professional hockey, while at the same time completing high school, collegial, or university education.

About 50 percent of those players that complete their junior training period with the league carry on to complete a university, professional, or technical education. Each year, the QMJHL grants more than $350,000 in scholarships, to over a hundred of its graduates. The specific scholarship amount per player depends on the policy of each league team.

http://theqmjhl.ca/

The NCAA versus CHL team scholarships

Participation in the NCAA recruitment process means a student-athlete is keen to gain a college degree while, at the same time, playing hockey at the college level.

The NCAA boasts of its ability to get student-athletes into the NHL via-à-vis other league options. Currently, the NCAA reports that 25 percent of NHL hockey recruits, from the past three years, came through the NCAA college system.

Compare the end-results:

Over 90% of NCAA hockey alumni go on to earn college degrees, while only about 20% of CHL alumni go on to do the same.

Facts about the CHL route

- Less than 2 percent of CHL first- and second rounders will ever play in the NHL
- For the past 5 years, only 3 percent of all CHL players have made it to the NHL
- During the 2007-2008 season, approximately 25 percent of NHL players came from the NCAA
- There were 33 NCAA players in the last two Stanley Cup Finals

How is the CHL different from the NCAA?

According to the NCAA, there are clear reasons for favouring the NCAA route over a CHL route. The most important reason is that the NCAA allows its student-athletes an average of six years over which they can study and develop as professional hockey players. The CHL offers its student-athletes between two to three years.

Note that each CHL team can only keep three 20-year-olds on their roster, which decreases the development time for young hockey players.

By contrast, the NCAA offers its student-athletes a six year guaranteed window in which to develop their hockey and academic skills.

- Those six years include two years of Junior or Prep School hockey followed by 4 years of college-level hockey.

NATIONAL ASSOCIATION OF INTERCOLLEGIATE ATHLETICS (NAIA) AND JUNIOR COLLEGES

If you are considering attending one of the junior colleges, or a small American university, which is not a part of the NCAA Division I, II, or III conferences, you may consider taking a look at the financial aid opportunities offered by the National Association of Intercollegiate Athletics (NAIA).

JumpForward strongly recommends student-athletes not get tunnel-vision for the NCAA and take a look at the opportunities in the NAIA, NJCAA, and other associations.

The NAIA caters to student-athletes who are looking to study at smaller colleges and universities. There are more than 300 NAIA associated colleges and universities across the United States and Canada. For a full listing of those schools, visit the NAIA website, as pictured below:

http://www.naia.org/ViewArticle.dbml?ATCLID=205322922

jumpforward.com and The Playbook break down the NAIA and other associations in detail.

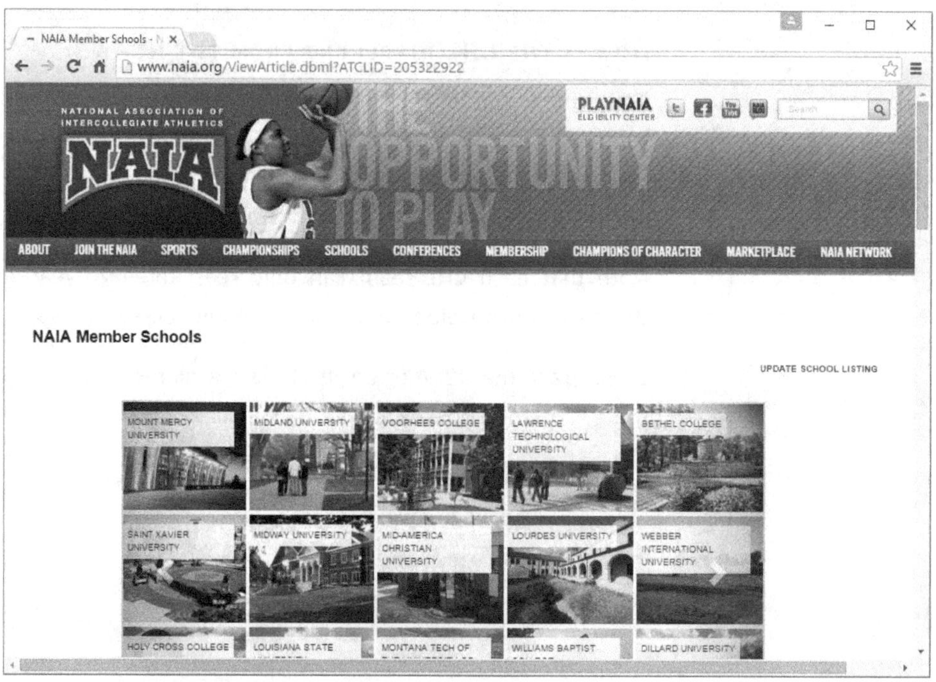

History of the NAIA

In the 1940s, the National Association of Intercollegiate Basketball (NAIB) came into existence in Kansas City, Missouri, where it hosted its first organizing convention. Three Kansas City businesspeople were responsible for forming the NAIB; they included Emil S. Liston, Dr. James Naismith, and Frank Cramer. As a group, the three business leaders decided to provide Kansas City fans with amateur competition. They also wanted to provide a mechanism by which smaller colleges and universities could develop national basketball champions.

In 1952, as a result of widespread demand from its member colleges, the NAIB expanded to become the National Association of Intercollegiate Athletics (NAIA), which encompassed a variety of sports. Since then, the NAIA has dedicated itself to fair, equitable, and accessible athletics for students from all socio-economic and sports backgrounds. The NAIA states, as part of its mandate, that it is committed to "academic achievement above athletic excellence" so student-athletes can succeed in their professional careers, after university. The organization considers itself to be a "trailblazer in providing equal opportunities for all student-athletes." The NAIA was the first American sporting conference to welcome in historically black colleges in the 1950s, and women's athletics teams in 1980.

The association now provides opportunities for more than 45,000 student-athletes, who are looking to achieve academic success while also competing in their chosen sport. The NAIA member institutions award millions of dollars through athletic aid to eligible student-athletes.

NAIA Eligibility Rules

If entering as a freshman, you must be a graduate of an accredited high school or be accepted as a regular student in good standing as defined by the enrolling institution and meet two of the three entry level requirements.

A) Achieve a minimum of 860 on the SAT or 18 on the ACT. The SAT score of 860 or higher must be calculated from the Critical Reading and Math scores only.

B) Achieve a minimum overall high school grade point average of 2.0 on a 4.0 scale.

C) Graduate in the top half of your high school graduating class.

For a complete and up-to-date list of NAIA eligibility requirements, please consult

http://www.playnaia.org/eligibility-center

Eligibility requirements for the NAIA

The NAIA has fewer recruiting restrictions as compared to the NCAA, especially with regards to academic requirements. For instance, the general high school eligibility rules for the NAIA boil down to the requirements stipulated in the box on the previous page. In addition, if you are a student-athlete who is planning to head to a two-year college to start your higher education, the NAIA can help you transfer to a four-year college team.

Contact the NAIA office using the information below, in order to find out how they can facilitate your transfer and even help you to find athletic scholarships to fund your further studies. This site also provides a link to the eligibility requirements for accessing NAIA scholarships and financial aid:

http://www.naia.org/ViewArticle.dbml?DB_OEM_ID=27900&ATCLID=205322931

Benefits of NAIA membership

A supportive environment can lead to success.
When you choose to attend one of, nearly, 300 NAIA member colleges or universities throughout the United States and Canada, you are welcomed into a supportive environment of students and faculty that are likely to become lifelong friends. Small classes, and closer student-faculty interaction, make it easy to form strong friendships with classmates and faculty, which could have a great impact on your success and career preparation.

Big opportunities are on smaller campuses.
With smaller campus communities, there are more opportunities for students to participate in activities. There are greater possibilities for students to experience leadership roles in student organizations, academics and intramural, and intercollegiate athletics. The NAIA offers 23 championships in 13 sports, and more than 90% of NAIA schools offer athletic scholarships.

You'll enjoy life outside the classroom with the variety of activities, athletic events, and religious services found at NAIA schools.

Champions of Character can brighten your future
The NAIA launched the Champions of Character program in 2000, to help students build character through sport. Promoting values like respect, responsibility, integrity, servant leadership, and sportsmanship. The NAIA Champions of Character program can help you make choices in all aspects of your life.

The program's community outreach component will help you connect with local employers and organizations that support the NAIA's character development initiative. This can help you gain valuable experience as an undergraduate, that prepares you for a successful career.

http://naia.cstv.com/member-services/students/

National Junior College Athletic Association (NJCAA)

In addition to the NCAA divisions and the NAIA colleges and universities, there is also the **National Junior College Athletic Association (NCJAA)**, which constitutes the primary option for student-athletes who are looking to attend community (also known as "junior") colleges in the United States. You can find the website at: http://www.njcaa.org/

The NJCAA is the governing body that regulates intercollegiate athletics for two-year colleges. Its programs are designed to meet the needs of the diverse group of students who have chosen to start their university careers at a two-year college, and who may be intending to move on to a four-year college in the future.

The NCJAA states that its mission is to:

Promote and foster junior college athletics on intersectional and national levels so that results will be consistent with the total educational program of its members.

As with the NCAA and the NAIA, the NJCAA aims to aid student-athletes in their academic careers, both financially and institutionally, in order to allow them to keep playing their favourite sports throughout their post-secondary education.

For eligibility information, consult the **NCJAA Eligibility Centre**, located at the following web address:

http://www.njcaa.org/eligibility/index

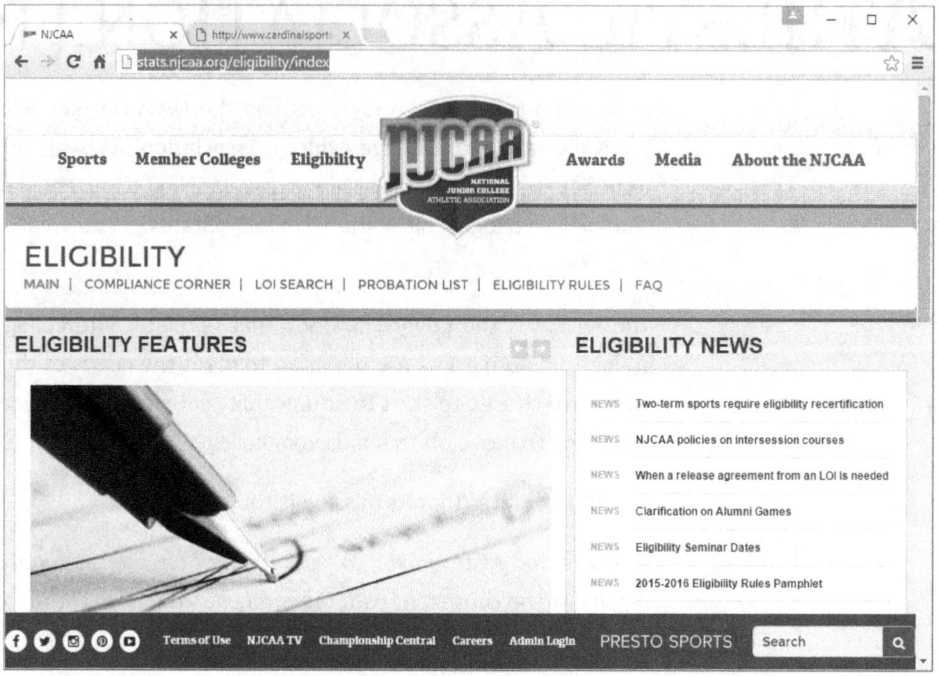

A full listing of all of the junior colleges that are members of the NCJAA can be found on their college listing website, located at:

http://www.njcaa.org/member_colleges/college-directory

www.jumpforward.com and The Playbook have detailed information on the NJCAA as well as other associations as part of the suite of tools and resources available to student-athletes.

COLLEGES | HIGH SCHOOL | CLUBS | BLOG | MEDIA | FEATURES | SITE INFO | LEARN MORE

NJCAA Recruiting Information

The Basics

National Junior College Athletic Association (NJCAA) serves as the governing body for 510 two year community colleges, junior college athletic departments, athletic conferences, and organizations. Rules and guidelines are developed for athletics eligibility and athletics competition for each of the three NJCAA divisions. NJCAA offers competition in the following 17 sports.

The Divisions

- Div. I
- Div. II
- Div. III

Scholarship Opportunities

Differences among the three divisions include scholarship availability. NJCAA Division I and Division II schools MAY offer athletic scholarships, whereas, Division III schools may NOT offer athletic scholarships. However, Division III schools can still OFFER many prospective Division III athletes SCHOLARSHIPS based on academics or financial need.

Divisional Scholarship Ammounts

- Div. I - A maximum of tuition and fees, room and board, course related books and transportation costs one time per academic

Contact

Address	1755 Telstar Drive Suite 103 Colorado Springs, CO 80920-0
Phone	719-590-7324
Fax	719-590-9788

Links

Main Web Site
NJCAA Eligibility Rules
NJCAA Amateur Guidelines
Information for a Prospective NJCAA Student-Athlete Guide
NJCAA Amateurism Questionnaire
NJCAA eligibility forms

Sports

SPORT	GENDER	SEASON
Cross Country	Men	Fall
Football	Men	Fall
Soccer	Men	Fall
Cross Country	Women	Fall

NJCAA National Office
1631 Mesa Avenue, Colorado Springs, CO 80906
Phone: 719.590.9788
Fax: 719.590.7324

Disclaimer: The information provided here is up-to-date as of printing date. Always check the NJCAA official website for the most accurate contact information.
http://www.njcaa.org/about/staff-directory

National Officers

Mary Ellen Leicht
Executive Director
meleicht@njcaa.org

Mark Krug
Assistant Executive Director
mkrug@njcaa.org

Brian Beck
Assistant Executive Director
bbeck@njcaa.org

Wanda Bodey
Associate Director of Compliance
wbodey@njcaa.org

Lorna Brizzie
Administrative Assistant/Bookkeeper
lbrizzie@njcaa.org

Dee DuBois
Administrative Assistant
ddubois@njcaa.org

Sarah Hoormann
Compliance Assistant
shoormann@njcaa.org

ATHLETIC RECRUITMENT: CARDINAL SPORTS MANAGEMENT GROUP

Cardinal Sports Management Inc. is a private recruitment management company that was established in 1994. It caters to student-athletes, teams, leagues, and associations, by providing services to those student-athletes who are interested in pursuing athletic scholarships, or financial aid packages, in order to attend post-secondary institutions in Canada and the United States. Cardinal Sports states that its mission is to:

"Provide student-athletes with the promotional support and career guidance required to achieve their athletic and academic goals."

Cardinal Sports conducts extensive interviews with potential student-athletes, and their families, in order to determine their realistic goals and objectives as athletes, and as students. Cardinal Sports will also complete an academic review of students in order to determine whether they meet all the NCAA eligibility requirements for differing divisions (including GPA analysis).

jumpforward.com

Amateurism Status Warning

When dealing with NCAA Division I and II Universities in particular, make sure you are the only one representing your talent to college coaches. You will lose your amateur status by having someone else make the direct contact with college coaches.

Be sure to ask services, like Cardinal Sports Management Group, what steps they take to ensure your status will not be compromised. If you have any questions, consult the Eligibility Centre directly for a ruling, before acting. Such services provide valuable consultation, but as the saying goes, "You can never be too careful."

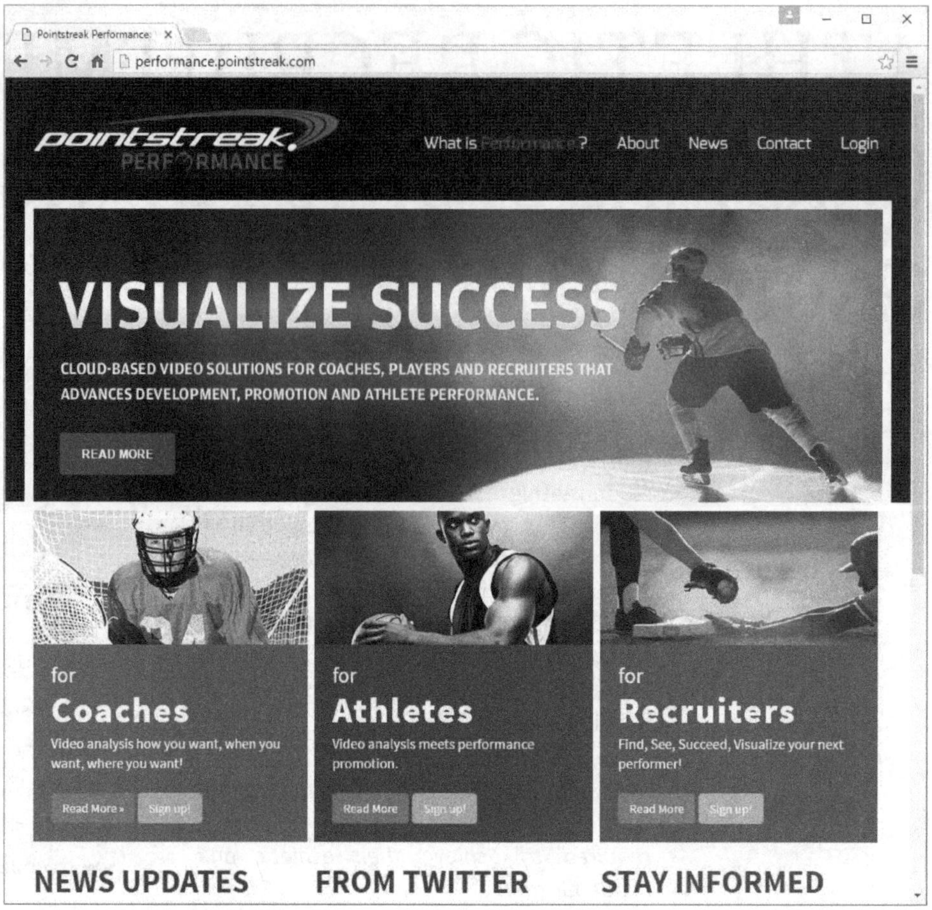

Cardinal Sports, which has been rebranded as Pointstreak Performance, has helped more than 2000 student-athletes secure scholarships and financial aid packages since its creation over two decades ago. It provides a network of representatives, throughout Canada and the United States, whose job it is to identify the best qualified student-athletes and get them competing at the collegiate level.

For more information about Cardinal Sports, and the various services it provides to individual student-athletes, consult the company's website:

http://performance.pointstreak.com

FINE ARTS APPLICANTS: THE NATIONAL PORTFOLIO DAY

The National Portfolio Day is an event organized specifically for visual artists and designers. It is an opportunity for prospective students, interested in pursuing an education in the visual and related arts, to meet with representatives from those colleges accredited by the National Association of Schools of Art and Design.

The National Portfolio Day is organized by the National Portfolio Day Association (NPDA), which was created in 1978 to facilitate the organization and planning of National Portfolio Days. The Association consists of representatives from those regionally accredited colleges and universities, that are members of the National Association of Schools of Art and Design. The NPDA states that its membership, *"represents the highest standard of visual arts education available in the United States and Canada."*

http://www.portfolioday.net/

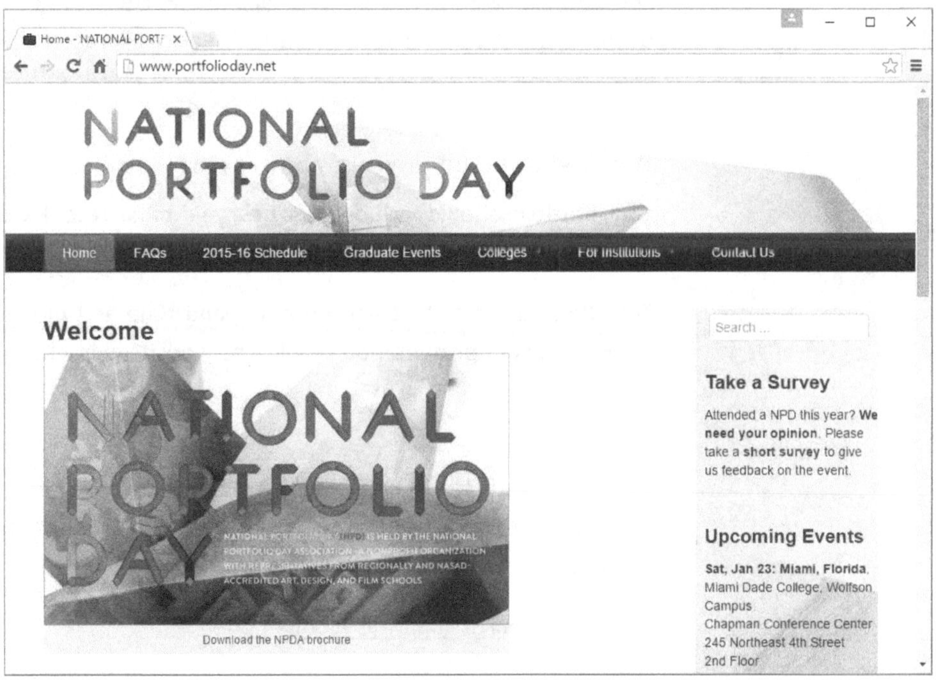

National Portfolio Day serves a number of purposes.

- It is designed to help further the artistic development of young artists by bringing together experienced college representatives to review their artwork and offer feedback.
- It exposes students and young artists to a variety of art forms and the world of professional art programs.
- It provides potential arts students with the opportunity to exchange information about their work, themselves, their college plans, and their concerns.

At the National Portfolio Day event you will find that college representatives are ready to discuss their respective programs with you; they are also prepared to critically discuss your artwork.

No admissions decisions or scholarship awards will be offered at the National Portfolio Day, although some college representatives may accept your portfolio as the visual portion of your application. Other colleges have restrictions that prohibit them from making a definite portfolio decision at the time of your review.

You **do not** have to register for a National Portfolio Day. All events are open to the public on a first-come-first-serve basis. They are all free of charge.

WHAT SHOULD BE IN YOUR PORTFOLIO?

Your portfolio should include your **best** and **most recent work**, but it can also include works in progress, sketchbooks and tear sheets.

The **NPDA** suggests that you do not spend time and money matting or framing your work. Keep your presentation simple; the work itself is what is of interest to the NPDA.

NATIONAL PORTFOLIO DAY SCHEDULE

Consult the NPDA's website for an up-to-date schedule of NPD events across North America:

http://www.portfolioday.net/component/

COLLEGE ADMISSIONS CONSULTANCY

Many students will appeal to a college consultant in order to ensure they apply to the institutions most suited to their needs and desires (note that "consultants" are sometimes also referred to as "private counsellors").

College consultants ensure students complete their entry applications properly, and submit their applications on time. They can also help to ensure the content of the application represents the student's full skills set. For those students who are looking to enter highly specific programs, or who are seeking scholarships based on particular skills (i.e. fine arts, sports, or other specialised skills), a college consultant can be helpful in ensuring the student accesses all services and resources available to them. Students who are looking to gain entry to Ivy Leagues schools may also want to consider hiring a consultant, in order to ensure their application caters to the particular student "identity" or "profile" that each Ivy League school sets out as being characteristic of its student body.

The following is a list of reasons for why you may choose to hire a consultant/private counsellor:

- Your school counsellor is focused on Canadian universities and does not possess information specific to the application processes for American colleges and universities.
- Your school counsellor is unable to give you the attention you require, either due to a high caseload or for any other reason.
- Your counsellor is pushing you to apply to particular "pet" schools that he/she prefers, despite the fact the school(s) in question are not appropriate fits.
- Your counsellor is unfamiliar with the particular type of college that you want to apply to (i.e. specialty colleges, such as liberal arts colleges).
- You do not get along with your counsellor and you are not confident that you will get fair treatment from him/her.

Tips on hiring consultants/private counsellors:

- Research the consultant's credentials and ask for references from past clients, before agreeing to pay for their services.
- Be wary of anyone who promises any sort of "success rate" or "guaranteed entry."
- Do not hire consultants who offer to do all the work for you (including application writing); this could lead to your immediate disqualification in the application process, especially if you are interviewed and the college suspects that you did not author your own application.
- Contact PREPSKILLS® for a recommended list of consultants.

US COLLEGE EXPO

Learn about the U.S. college admissions process and speak to the U.S. college admissions teams themselves at the US College Expo, which is held in April/May every year!

ONLINE RESOURCE INDEX

College Extras

www.prepskills.com
Provides SAT and ACT study preparation, prep classes and practice testing to aid students looking for American university admissions.

www.uscollegeexpo.com
Canada's unique, annual US College Expo that exclusively features American colleges. Supporting Canadian students who are considering US educational options.

www.u101.com
Provides a listing of American colleges, including online and distance learning colleges.

www.collegenet.com
Provides over 1500 Internet admissions applications for colleges and universities.

www.collegenews.com
Allows you to interact with other college candidates; also allows you to create an online scholarship profile that can help you win money for school.

www.collegetoolkit.com
Provides college and scholarship search mechanisms; allows for career exploration options.

www.collegeconfidential.com/
Provides online discussions regarding college life, scholarships, financing and campuses.

www.commonapp.org
Provides admissions applications – online and in print – for 300 colleges.

www.fastweb.com
Provides a useful college search mechanism, as well as job and internship searches.

www.nces.ed.gov/collegenavigator
Provides comprehensive school listings and search criteria; allows you to search and compare profiles of over 7000 colleges and universities.

www.unigo.com
Provides college reviews submitted by current and former students.

www.utexas.edu/world/univ/state/
Provides college listings categorized by geographical location.

Counselling and consultancy

www.nacacnet.org
Provides information on private admissions counsellors in your area.

Financial aid and scholarship information

intlscholarships.googlepages.com/needbased
Provides a listing of financial aid and scholarships available for international students at American colleges.

student.collegeboard.org/css-financial-aid-profile
Allows you to create an online information form that member colleges use to distribute scholarship funds.

www.ammsa.com/content/national-scholarships
Provides a listing of scholarships for Aboriginal students.

collegereadiness.collegeboard.org/psat-nmsqt-psat-10/scholarships-and-recognition
Administers scholarships based on high PSAT scores for those students who come from Hispanic and Latino communities.

www.college-scholarships.com
Provides a general listing of colleges, scholarships and financial aid options.

www.fafsa.ed.gov
Provides comprehensive information regarding Federal Financial Aid, especially for American citizens (you can apply using the online application form).

www.finaid.org
Provides a comprehensive listing of various financial aid options.

www.servicecanada.gc.ca/eng/goc/cslp.shtml
Provides application information and materials for Canadian federal student loans.

www.educationusa.info
EducationUSA is a network of hundreds of advising centers in 170 countries, where millions of international students each year find accurate, comprehensive, and current information about how to apply to accredited U.S. colleges and universities.

www.mefa.org
Provides information on special, low-interest loans through the Massachusetts Educational Financing Authority (MEFA) for Canadian students looking to study at colleges in Massachusetts.

www.nasfaa.org
Provides comprehensive information for counsellors and students regarding funding options at American colleges (including information on FAFSA) through the National Association of Student Financial Aid Administrators (NASFAA)

www.nationalmerit.org
Provides information on scholarships based on high PSAT scores.

www.parentplusloan.com
Provides information for parents seeking a PLUS Loan for their teen student (you can apply for the PLUS loan using the online application form).

www.scholarships.com
A comprehensive listing of merit-based, need-based and specialty scholarships available in Canada and the United States. The site allows students to form a personal profile that is then used to direct scholarship options their way.

www.tdcanadatrust.com/scholarship/
Provides information on scholarships issued by TD Canada Trust for students attending post-secondary educational institutions in Canada and abroad.

www.tellurideassociation.org
Offers scholarships to gifted juniors who wish to take summer seminars in the humanities or social sciences.

Rankings

colleges.usnews.rankingsandreviews.com/best-colleges
U.S. News America's Best Colleges ranking.

www.forbes.com/education/
Forbes Magazine college ranking.

www.timeshighereducation.com/world-university-rankings/
Times Higher Education international college ranking.

www.washingtonmonthly.com/college_guide/
Washington Monthly's college ranking.

STANDARDIZED TESTS

www.prepskills.com

PREPSKILLS® provides preparation courses for the SAT, SAT subject tests, PSAT and ACT for students interested in American universities.

actstudent.org
Provides information on the ACT; allows you to register for the ACT online.

www.collegeboard.org
Provides information on the SAT and SAT Subject Tests; allows you to register online for the SAT and SAT Subject Tests.

collegereadiness.collegeboard.org/psat-nmsqt-psat-10
Provides information on the PSAT for students in Grade 10.

STUDENT-ARTISTS

www.portfolioday.net/
Provides information on National Portfolio Days for visual arts students.

STUDENT-ATHLETES

www.jumpforward.com
A featured partner of Prepskills that offers free recruiting tools and resources to high school student-athletes looking to make the jump to college.

www.athleticscholarships.net
Provides listings of potential scholarship opportunities for student-athletes.

http://performance.pointstreak.com
Offers recruitment services for student-athletes in Canada and the U.S.

www.eligibilitycenter.org
Serves as the eligibility centre for the NCAA, a site every prospective student-athlete interested in the NCAA must visit; provides information and application material related to student-athletes.

www.naia.org
Provides information for student-athletes looking to apply to smaller colleges.

www.nationalletter.org
Provides information on the National Letter of Intent for student-athletes applying for athletics funding through the NCAA.

www.ncaa.org
Provides information for students looking to gain entry to NCAA Division I, II and III colleges.

www.njcaa.org/todaysNJCAA_Eligibility.cfm?category=Eligibility
Provides information and application materials for student-athletes looking to attend two-year colleges.

VOLUNTEERING

www.globalroutes.org
Provides information on summer foreign exchange programs for high school students.

www.volunteermatch.org
Provides volunteer opportunities searchable by area, interest, and age range.

www.volunteersolutions.org
Connects individuals to volunteer opportunities within local communities.

Sample Admissions Essays

My Pet

The question of whether I have a pet is warranted in any amateur icebreaking conversation. My response is always, "Yes, I do; I have a little sister." Past the physical disparity, the two are not that different. They both crave attention, require daily playground time and necessitate careful potty-training.

My sister Feier and I are twelve years apart. (As such, I receive my fair share of "teenage mother" comments when I take her out.) Our lives spin on different axes. While I deliberate on the transcendental oversoul in The Grapes of Wrath for English class, Feier struggles with chapter books in the Hannah Montana series; while I speculate about the heat death of the universe during physics lectures, she dwells upon the intangible sum of five and seventeen. Yet, this divergence between us is endearing.

As part of her six-year-old birthday present, I gave her a kaleidoscope. Feier was thrilled. She walked about blindly for the next hour, with her left eye shut and her right cemented to the eye of the contraption. I reckoned that she was, just as I once was, awed by the perpetual flux in colour, design and light. With every rotation, Feier would gasp and exclaim, "Look!" as if we all had access to her latest masterpiece. I found her childish wonder nostalgic.

Two years ago, I wept silently over the loss of my best friend to the United States. Minutes later, I felt a small ball of warmth by my side and glanced up to find Feier convulsing with tears, her shoulders bowed and her face cupped in her tiny hands. I instinctively drew her to me and rocked her in my arms until the sobbing subsided. I inquired to the reason for her sadness. She looked up at me, her eyes still welling with residue tears, and said, "I don't know, I was only trying to help you cry."

Over the years, I have ambled into the shoes of Feier's role model. There have been hints to this. When she realized that I was the captain of the cheerleading team, she bought little bows for her hair and glitter for her eyes; when she attended my ballet recital, she donned a leotard and tights to sign up for her own dance classes; when she watched a video of me speaking at a corporate dinner for Kids Help Phone, she well, made a more salient effort to dominate our dinner conversations.

I remarked a week ago that I will be eighteen in three months.

"Wow," Feier breathed, "you're going to be a grown up!"

I must have seemed like the quintessence of a cool older sister then, ripening with maturity that she can hardly wait to grasp onto. Yet, as I watched Feier run away, no doubt to inform her friends how cool I was to be teetering on the threshold of maturity (not in those exact words), I mused; slow down, my pet, you have wonder on your side.

SUPPLEMENTARY – WRITE PAGE 217 OF YOUR AUTOBIOGRAPHY

Not sure if I would fit in with my new Spanish family. I mean, I didn't exactly think in purring r's.

Plates of Argentinean sausages paraded across from under my nose, sizzling in their own grease.

"*Chorizos*," enunciated my husband.

"*Cho-di-sos*?"

Sausage, *saucisse, sosej, shyang chung* and now *chorizo*... I secretly hoped that my linguistic prowess of knowing "sausage" in five languages would be vaguely impressive to my new mother-in-law. Putting fork to plate, I brought a ball of authentic Argentinean grill to my lips. It was delicious! Tumbling in the rotund vowels of *chorizo*, and oozing with the greasy sounds of *saucisse*, it was as if the flavours of its names had been rolled into its pith.

Earlier that evening, I stood atop the cottage patio and was awed by the Argentinean countryside. Treetops weaved an evergreen rug that blanketed all but the heaving mountains and lone wisps of silver smoke that drifted towards the snowy peaks. It looked like the backdrop of a fairytale. Consumed with the romance of the scenery, my husband and I broke out in bilingual duets to Sleeping Beauty. Melodies of French and Spanish bobbed on the thick dusky air. As Andres trolled in full oh'sand eh's, I accompanied in soft ah's and ai's. That night, the usually winsome Spanish sounds seemed oddly incongruous to the evening sweetness, especially when held to the dulcet French lulls. I thought, perhaps the soothing swells of the French language had a way of eliciting romance and beauty; perhaps the romance and beauty of the French had translated into their language. MySpanish-speaking husband was not amused that my revelations favoured the French.

In my affairs with foreign languages, I didn't always understand the content of the conversations, but from sounds and intonations, I managed to gather the general intent. I tried to explain to Andres that with languages, I may lose the words, but never the meaning.

Yet, words do embody meaning. When the wind whistled for nightfall that eve, I ambled backwards for the doorsill with my eyes still tangled in the horizon. Oh, how I envied Andres for growing up there. The setting sun, a slice of golden pie wedged between the mountain peaks, mesmerized me and something ineffable inclined me to linger. I grasped for that feeling. It was shapeless in the vocabulary of the romance languages but took form in Chinese. *Bu shuh* - it was the epitome of what I felt, a sense of longing and reluctance. They say thoughts transcend words, but I think that is chiefly because no language is comprehensive enough to denote our thoughts alone.

I grew up with different tongues. First acquainted with Chinese and English, I then flirted with Malay, Tamil and Hokkein when I lived in Singapore. During my teenage years, my Canadian citizenship added French to my repertoire and now, our trip to Argentina made Spanish my latest muse.

Andres has often asked me which language I think in. Like all worthwhile questions, there is more than one answer; I realized then that my thoughts are marinated in a potpourri of languages, steeped in the most pregnant of phrases from each. I find that each language, like gossamer, veils its words in an auxiliary tenor. There is romance to French, passion to Spanish, clarity to Chinese and dignity to English. Together, each compliment and compensate for what the other cannot express to fashion a broader mosaic of tangible thought.

I looked up from the chorizo at my new family, parleying across the dinner table in fervent Spanish. I foraged for a word to describe them. Warm and inviting, vivacious and bold, I thought they were beautiful. No, I thought: *eran hermosos*.

WHY UPENN?

I have recently managed to surprise several of my teachers. When I mentioned to my philosophy teacher that I thought high science to be as much rationalism as empiricism, he raised an eyebrow and said, "You do sciences?" When I teased my chemistry teacher saying that the literature head had better style than he did, he retorted in jest, "You take lit?" When I told my cheerleading coach that I will be missing practice for an AP exam, she laughed and said, "You're an AP student?" I inwardly rationalized that their unawareness to my potential is because I am simply too stellar in their respective disciplines.

Over the years, I have realized that my passion lies in a plethora of courses, and my gluttony for a buffet of knowledge brings me to the University of Pennsylvania. UPenn was founded on Benjamin Franklin's principles of innovation, pragmatic learning and well-rounded education. It offers an expansive selection of courses spanning all four undergraduate schools. Its unique one university concept ensures that even in the absence of a suitable preassembled major, all my interests shall be met. It is an appetizing offer because I like my major like a Wendy's burger – unique and named after me. The Dorcy major is bound to be organic. It is beefed up with biology, topped with creative ingredients like comparative literature and romance languages and sandwiched between thin servings of calculus and chemistry.

Yet despite its exceptional academic options, much of UPenn's appeal lies beyond its classrooms. There are numerous lecturers and amenities to be taken advantage of. The Centre for Programs in Contemporary Writing speaks to the language addict in me and the many research facilities appeal to my inner Curious George. Since young, I have learnt best through hands-on discovery for it is through guessing, fumbling, hoping, failing, and even more fumbling that I discover knowledge, and more importantly, the process to discovering knowledge. UPenn is home to some of the best research facilities around and I plan to capitalize on its resources, fully exploiting the Center for Undergraduate Research and Fellowships during my time on campus.

Adding further appeal, UPenn is ranked first in the Ivy League for international placements. Having lived in 3 countries, travelled to 12 and studied at 14 schools, I harbour a profound wanderlust. To me, travelling is more than a change in scenery, it is about personal challenges and that is exactly what UPenn offers. From athletics to student groups to Greek Life, UPenn is bubbling with challenging opportunities.

There must be more who champion what I rave as there are nearly 20 000 students within UPenn's doors. This impressive number brings diversity to fuel more than 300 student clubs and an animated social scene; it is what makes UPenn hot with energy. They say life at UPenn is sleep, work and play, but only two of the three. I say, give me a blended smoothie of all three because my passion for education and college life is too grand to be contained in two.

While there are other schools that offer liberal arts programs, only UPenn does it with such novelty and vivacity. If Benjamin Franklin's electrifying approach to knowledge is any indication of the school he has founded, I am sure sparks will fly at UPenn.

Up & Down

It's one of those crisp autumn days. The kind that makes me realize why autumn is my favorite season. There is a cool taste to the air, crunchy leaves all over the ground and far away birds flying in V-formations. It gets chilly every time the wind blows in my direction but even pain is welcome when it signifies autumn. Not too many people are out right now, only three teenage boys throwing around a basketball and a brittle grandpa raking his scattered leaves before the first snowfall. After a few minutes of walking up this same, uniform street, I reach a short metal fence, and now I'm here.

There are monkey bars. There are three different slides. There is even a sand pit. But my eyes completely ignore these other attractions and head straight for the swings. They are rusted and squeaky, but it doesn't matter because they are *my* swings. I wiggle in place on the cold piece of black plastic and start pumping my legs. There's no one around to push me but I'm excited to put the skill I have been practicing since preschool to use.

And then I cry. I cry because my best friends are hundreds of miles away. I cry because my dad is just as far. I cry because I know no one at my new school. I cry because my mom has been diagnosed with breast cancer. I let myself drain.

But then I stop and dream. And that is when autumn really becomes autumn. Up, down, up down. I open my eyes and I can see the clouds. Fluffy, gorgeous clouds right above my head with golden rays peaking through the cracks. True signs of a perfect sunset. I never look down. Why would I when there is such a beautiful sight in front of me? The real treat then shows itself when I close my eyes and squeeze my tears away.

Even though everything is black, I can see the autumn sunset scene as if my eyes were still open. Not only that, but I see other images as well. Everything is as clear as the biting breeze. All the thoughts, worries and problems that have been soaring through my head are being painted on this black canvas. I can feel myself falling face first with my hair flying behind me, but then being brought back up towards the sky with the sun shining on my face.

I go to these swings every day. It has been two years since I moved and now, I smile. I smile because I'm still close to my best friends. I smile because my dad is here visiting. I smile because I have met so many new friends. I smile because my mom has become a stronger woman. When I feel like I'm falling face first to the ground, I know that if I keep working my legs, I'll be in the sky again soon. This has become how I live my life. Today, I smile because I am happy.

Graduate School Admissions Essays

The Essay

Many graduate schools require a personal essay or personal statement that describes who you are and what your primary objectives in life are. These essays can seem difficult to write, especially given that they should help to set your application apart from everyone else's.

Some basic rules to follow in producing a top quality essay include the following:

a) Be specific

A generic essay which talks about abstract and undefined concepts such as "I want to improve myself," "I want to contribute to the community," or "I want to be a leader" will not impress the admissions team. If those sentiments do in fact reflect how you feel about yourself, or your upcoming graduate experience, you need to make them more concrete by offering detailed and specific examples related to what you have done in the past, or what you plan to do in the future. Whether you choose to write an essay that highlights your personal goals and objectives, or one that discusses a general theme (as chosen by the school), providing detailed examples is the best means of setting your essay apart from everyone else's.

RULE: ***Avoid generalizations; offer only specifics.***

b) Clean copy

Always make sure to edit, re-edit, and edit your essay one more time, before you submit it as part of your application. Remember, no matter how many times you read your own essay, you will miss some grammatical and syntactical points. Always have a parent, friend, or professor proof-read your final copy before submitting it.

RULE: ***Everyone needs an editor; get one.***

c) Follow the rules

If an application says "500 words," only write five-hundred words. Don't think you're above the rules governing applications. At best, extra words will simply be ignored; at worst, admissions staff will take it to be an indication that you do not follow academic standards when they are stipulated. Don't do yourself a disservice: follow the rules stipulated by the application, and do not write more or less than what is required of you.

There is one caveat to this rule. If an application suggests a range, say "300 to 500 words," always aim for the upper end of the range, but do not exceed it. In such an instance, it is in your benefit to write 499 words about the essay topic. If you can include one extra example to highlight your point, or solidify your argument, do so.

RULE: ***Word lengths are non-negotiable, but aim for the upper limit.***

Typical Application Essay Questions

No two graduate schools are the same when it comes to posing application essay questions. But because the application process is such a grand and universalizing one, there are some typical types of questions you will see posed on your admissions application.

Start to think about how you would go about answering such questions. In preparing your thoughts, keep in mind that these essays are like all other essays in that you must have an introduction, a body, and a conclusion.

Here is a list of some real graduate school essay questions. They demonstrate some typical question types:

- Describe your most rewarding or unrewarding educational experience.
- Ask and answer your own question.
- Write a page of your own autobiography.
- Discuss an issue of personal, local, national, or international concern and its importance to you.
- Indicate a person who has had a significant influence on you and describe that influence.
- How do you see the world in 2020?
- Describe how a song, poem, piece of art, book, etc., influenced your life.
- Select two ideals listed in our literature and relate them to your personal beliefs and convictions.
- Evaluate a significant experience or achievement that has special meaning to you.
- How have you taken something you've learned in the class room and integrated it into your non-academic life?
- If you could meet anyone, real or imaginary, who would it be?
- How will your knowledge of other cultures affect your studies?
- Describe a situation in which your values were challenged.
- Pick a recent event and relate it to a turning point in your life.
- Describe an experience that illustrates a proverb, maxim, or quote that has special meaning for you?
- Relate your future goals to studying at our school.
- Describe an ethical dilemma that you have faced and how you have resolved it.

Score Choice – How many times should you write your SAT?

By Joanna Severino, President of PREPSKILLS® Inc.
Published in Spring/Summer 2010 of Canadian Student Magazine
Revised in Spring 2016 to reflect changes to the SAT

The College Board introduced Score Choice – much to the delight of students worldwide, many of whom believed it had just made applying to American universities and colleges a lot easier. Score Choice is a policy that relates to the SAT Reasoning Test—a test that students must write to gain admission to 80% of American colleges. In the past, the College Board (the non-profit organization that administers and runs the SAT) has stipulated that if a student writes the SAT repeatedly, *all* of their scores would necessarily be sent to colleges as part their admissions application. With the introduction of Score Choice just over a year ago, the situation has changed dramatically.

The College Board introduced the policy of "Score Choice" in order to provide students with the opportunity to choose which SAT scores they report on their college admissions applications.

Prima facie, Score Choice sounds like a great policy all around—a transformation in score reporting that ultimately favours the student. Consider the new scenario: you can now write, and rewrite, and rewrite, and rewrite some more...until you got the score that you want. In fact, the only limitation to your rewrites is the number of exam sessions each calendar year (there are only six in Canada).

In this new Score Choice world, you can, in theory, pick your highest scores from a plethora of possible SAT sittings. No one will ever know that you might have scored a 1000 (out of a possible 1600) on your first try given that you later scored 1500 (you only have to report the second score).

Not surprisingly, many students (and their parents) thought the new Score Choice policy had just made getting into American colleges a lot easier.

Unfortunately, Score Choice has created a more complicated admissions world than students first realize.

There are two reasons why.

The first is that Score Choice is a College Board policy, which individual colleges and universities can choose to opt in or out of. Individual universities and colleges devise yearly policies towards Score Choice reporting, and many of them have rejected Score Choice.

For instance, when Score Choice first appeared in late 2008, a number of Ivy League universities and top state schools boldly declared they wouldn't accept it. The University of Pennsylvania, Stanford, Columbia and Cornell all continued to require that students submit every SAT score on their exam transcript. Failure to do so disqualified a student's admission application.

This meant that students who plan to apply to multiple universities and colleges need to be careful about whether they chose to rewrite the exam at all, let alone rewrite it repeatedly. Multiple rewrites do not look good on an admissions application, and if your college rejects Score Choice, then you must report all scores (including your poor scores).

The second reason Score Choice has hindered some students' performances is that it has added to the mythical view that by simply rewriting the SAT (i.e. without doing anything to improve upon SAT-specific skills or test-taking strategies), a student can increase her score. This is not the case. Studies analyzing the behaviour of students who rewrite standardized exams indicate that repeat exam sessions do not improve scores. In fact, among one-third of students, scores actually decrease over repeat sessions. This is because standardized exams are designed to make students score within a certain bandwidth. If a student's first score on the SAT is 1000, their second score won't be far off – especially if they do nothing to target their test-taking skills in the interim.

Learning SAT-specific test-taking skills is the only way to improve a SAT score. The best bet, therefore, is to learn these skills *before* you ever sit down to take the exam.

What to do?

Rather than worrying about whether you should rewrite the SAT, PREPSKILLS recommends that students "Do it once, do it right!" To succeed on the SAT, start with these steps:

1) Plan to enrol in an SAT-specific training course with a Canadian provider – i.e. a company, like PREPSKILLS, that specializes in sending Canadian students abroad. Canadian companies know where the curriculum differs between American and Canadian high schools. These courses generally take 8 to 12 weeks, depending on your skills levels. So plan ahead!
2) Learn about the SAT-specific scoring penalty, which penalizes you for incorrect answers. PREPSKILLS analyzes a student's score range to figure out the degree to which this penalty is artificially hurting a student's score. If you are unaware of the scoring penalty, take some time looking at the College Board website (www.collegeboard.org) to learn more about it.
3) Plan to write your SAT at the end of Grade 10 or in Grade 11. Do not leave it until Grade 12. If you leave it until Grade 12, it might be too late to meet early admissions deadlines for your college.

For more information on preparatory training services for the SAT visit www.prepskills.com . Courses are delivered in class within the Greater Toronto Area and online via distance learning options for other Canadian locations.

College ranking tables: how do you know which college is the best?

By Joanna Severino, President of PREPSKILLS® Inc.

Various private organizations within the United States and globally generate annual or periodic college ranking tables. Those tables are supposed to provide readers with a list of the best and worst universities and colleges in the U.S.

In theory, a prospective student should be able to consult such ranking tables in order to decide which schools offer the best education in a particular area of study.

Unfortunately, things are not so simple. Each organization uses a range of diverse statistical measures to generate its respective tables, some of which may produce rankings that are entirely irrelevant to a student's academic interests.

Canadian students who are looking to apply to American colleges and universities should therefore be wary of the differing statistical methodologies used to generate ranking tables.

Some of the factors considered in generating a ranking list include (but are not restricted to) class sizes, range of degree options, specificity of degree options, opportunities for internships, scholarships and bursaries, peer review publications and research output, existence of technical degrees (such as law, medicine and business administration), financial success of alumni, and student, alumni and professor surveys.

The list below is composed of some of the most popular college rankings. Here you will find a number of ranking systems along with a brief description of the measures that each system uses to distinguish between top-performing colleges.

U.S. News America's Best Colleges (annual ranking) ranks national universities, liberal arts colleges, business programs and engineering programs. U.S. News uses a variety of indicators that are supposed to "capture academic quality," the organization says. According to U.S. News, those indicators fall into the following seven categories: assessment by administrators at peer institutions, retention of students, faculty resources, student selectivity, financial resources, alumni giving, and "graduation rate performance," which refers to the difference between the proportion of students who are expected to graduate and the proportion of students who actually do.

U.S. News feels that its ranking tables tell students and parents how well an "institution does its job of educating students."

However, U.S. News admits that "many factors other than those we measure will figure in your decision, including the feel of campus life, activities, sports, academic offerings, location, cost, and availability of financial aid." None of those items are included in the U.S. News rankings.

In 2009, US News ranked Harvard University as the number one university. For more information on the U.S. News rankings, visit their website at http://colleges.usnews.rankingsandreviews.com/college

The Washington Monthly's "College Rankings" produced a controversial, though comprehensive, report in 2005 (published in 2006) entitled "Is our students learning?" That

report offered American university and college rankings based upon how well the college had performed as an engine for social mobility. The surveyors researched whether colleges helped poor student get rich and educated or whether they just helped rich students stay rich and get even more educated. Washington Monthly's ranking also considered the degree to which colleges fostered scientific and humanistic research that aimed at improving society through the promotion of an ethic of public service. Washington Monthly reported that the Massachusetts Institute of Technology (MIT) emerged as the number one college in the United States based on those measures. http://www.washingtonmonthly.com/features/2006/0609.collegechart.html

Forbes magazine online (Forbes.com) published a list of "America's Best Colleges" in 2008. In association with the Centre for College Affordability and Productivity, Forbes used an Alumni Who's Who in America, student evaluations at www.ratemyprofessors.com, four-year graduation rates, enrolment-adjusted numbers of students and faculty who had received nationally competitive awards, and four-year accumulated student debt as its indicators. Forbes also separated colleges into top "overall," "public" and "private" schools.

The college that topped Forbes's "overall" listing was Princeton University, which also topped its "private" school category. The college that topped Forbes's "public" listing was the United States Military Academy. http://bestcollegerankings.org/popular-rankings/forbes-college-rankings/

The Times Higher Education, a British publication that reports on higher education news, in association with Quacquarelli Symonds, publish the THES - QS World University Rankings—a listing of 500 universities from around the world. The list included many more non-American universities (especially British schools) in its upper tier of top colleges and universities. The THES - QS ranking uses a "peer review" system that incorporates the views of more than 3000 scholars and academics working in various research fields. In 2008, the Times Higher ranked Harvard as its number one university. At the end of this year, Quacquarelli Symonds will be reviewing its measures and methodology for future rankings. http://www.timeshighereducation.co.uk/world-university-rankings/

Students and parents should use these ranking tables with caution. They can be useful tools as they can help students identify colleges and universities that they would not have otherwise thought to consider. However, determining which college or university will be best suited for any particular student includes considering a wide range of factors.

Each of the rankings discussed above does not, and cannot, incorporate the personal needs of any one student. Thus, rankings are best understood as subjective tools rather than absolute guides.

PREPSKILLS®
INC

876 Eglinton Ave East
Toronto, Ontario
M4G 2L1

Phone: 416-200-7728
Toll Free: 1-866-973-7737
Fax: 416-423-0932
Email: info@prepskills.com
www.PREPSKILLS.com

PREPSKILLS® U.S. Admissions Workshop

Applying to American colleges? If so, there are probably a lot of questions you need answered.

- How do colleges determine who gets in and who gets denied?
- What sort of funding is there for Canadian students?
- What is the difference between **early decision** and **early action** admissions?
- What are the **Ivy League schools** looking for?
- What do **student-athletes** need to do?

To provide you with answers to all of these questions (and more), PREPSKILLS® has developed the **PREPSKILLS® U.S. College Admissions Workshop**, a one-on-one consultation with Joanna Severino, the Founder and President of PREPSKILLS®.

Applying for entry to an American college is a **two-year process**, and it can be a **three-year process** if you decide to take the PSAT! It's best to be prepared ahead of time, rather than finding yourself overwhelmed by obligations, stipulations, and specific requirements that you can't meet in Grade 12.

Ensure that you are prepared to submit your application successfully. Contact PREPSKILLS® today to register for the **PREPSKILLS® US College Admissions workshop**.

PREPSKILLS® U.S. College Admissions Workshop Curriculum

Materials	The ***Admissions Guide for Canadian Students*** includes information on the following: • Types of American colleges (e.g. Ivy League, liberal arts, community college) • PSAT/SAT/ACT testing requirements • College rankings and methodological considerations • Ivy League and top college specificities and requirements • Diversifying applications for admissions officers • Scholarships, loans and financing for Canadian students • Financial aid case studies • NCAA and student-athlete considerations • National Portfolio Days and student-artist considerations
Workshop Overview	Prior to attending the **Admissions Workshop**, participants will be asked to: • Identify their **top two college choices** • Complete a **Common Application admission essay** (to be submitted to PREPSKILLS® two days in advance of the workshop) • Complete a **Personal Attributes Worksheet** listing extra-curricular activities. During the workshop, participants will: • Complete a **Steps To Gain Admission** task-list and timeline • Complete an **Interview Skills Analysis** worksheet
Workshop Consultancy Services	At the **Workshop**, participants will receive individualized and group consultancy on: • College "fit" (for selected colleges) • Student profiling • Admission essay commentary and analysis • Standardized testing (i.e. SAT and ACT) analysis • High school G.P.A. (Grade Point Average) profiling • Interview tips and commentary • NCAA overview and admissions profiling

prepskills®
ADVANCED PREPARATION. ENDLESS OPPORTUNITY.™

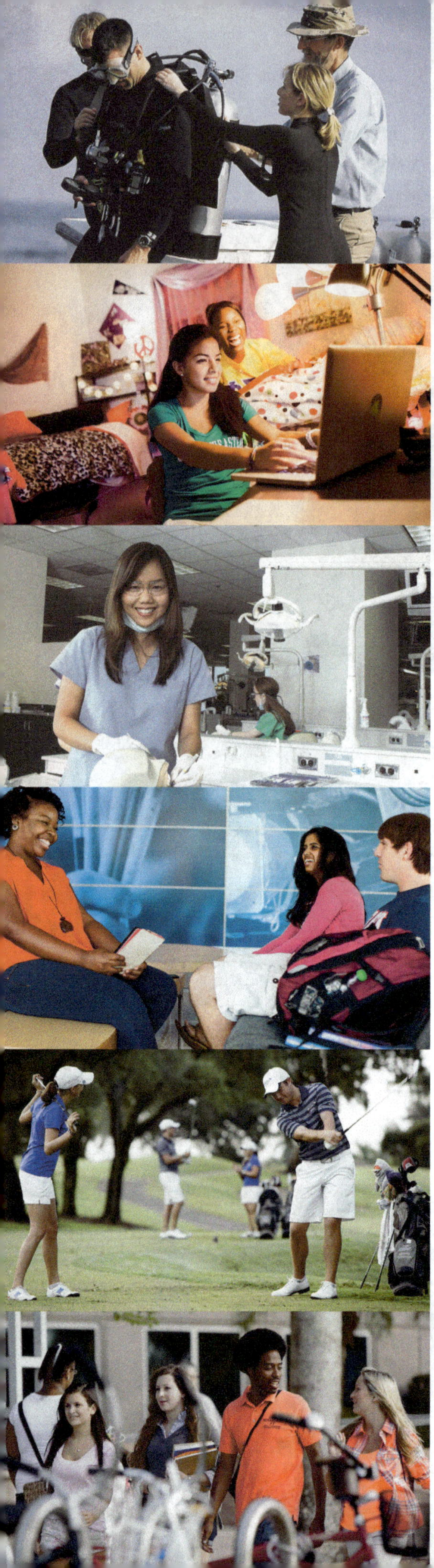

$1 MILLION
in INTERNATIONAL SCHOLARSHIPS
RANKED 50
in the WORLD
for ALUMNI EMPLOYMENT
Center for World University Rankings, 2015
#68 BEST
GLOBAL UNIVERSITIES
Center for World University Rankings, 2015
TOP COLLEGE
BEST REGIONAL COLLEGE FOR THE WEST
Princeton Review 2015
Discover a university where academic quality, state-of-the-art research, and community are vital parts of your educational experience. Offering a world-class education and a beautiful campus-setting, it's no surprise that students from over 116 countries enroll at the University of Arizona each year.
Find out more today!
admissions.arizona.edu/international
THE UNIVERSITY OF ARIZONA
STAY CONNECTED:
intladmissions@email.arizona.edu
instagram.com/uaadmissions
twitter.com/uaadmissions
fb.com/uarizona
THE UNIVERSITY OF ARIZONA

Where potential
BECOMES POSSIBILITY.
oakland.edu
OAKLAND UNIVERSITY

SANTA ROSA JUNIOR COLLEGE

Beautiful, Safe Sonoma County
- Diverse, welcoming community
- Relaxed, rural environment
- First 2 years of bachelor's degree

Popular Majors

- Agriculture Sciences
- Business
- Communication
- Computer Sciences
- Culinary Arts
- Electronics
- Engineering
- Fine Arts
- Health Sciences
- Journalism
- Life Sciences
- Political Science
- Social Sciences
- STEM

Quick Facts

- 20,000 full-time students
- Student to faculty ratio – 19 to 1
- Over 100 majors
- Over 150 certificate programs
- Competitive sports

Semester	Application Deadline
Summer 2017	April 24, 2017
Fall 2017	June 8, 2017
Spring 2018	November 2017

Transfer Facts

- SRJC is #1 in UC acceptance rates among the larger California community colleges.
- SRJC has transfer agreements with 4-year universities, making it easy to transfer.
- Top transfer destinations for SRJC students are: UC Berkeley, UC Davis, UC Santa Cruz, Sonoma State University, San Francisco State University.
- Students can transfer to universities throughout the U.S.

Estimated Student Expenses for Academic Year

SRJC Tuition Fees (based on 24 units per year @ $303 per unit) (Tuition and Fees are subject to change)	$7,300
Mandatory school fees	$50
Living Expenses (housing/room and board)	$12,000
Books & Supplies	$1,800
Miscellaneous costs (transportation, personal expenses, clothing)	$2,050
SRJC Medical Insurance	$1,800
Total Expenses	$25,000

Contact Information

Santa Rosa Junior College
1501 Mendocino Avenue
Santa Rosa, California USA 95401
"Like us" on Facebook – SRJC International Student Program

Discrimination Disclaimer: The Sonoma County Junior College District does not discriminate on the basis of race, religious creed, color, national origin, ancestry, ethnic group identification, physical disability, mental disability, medical condition, genetic condition, marital status, sex, gender, gender identity, gender expression, genetic information or sexual orientation in any of its policies, procedures or practices; nor does the District discriminate against any employees or applicants for employment on the basis of their age. This non-discrimination policy covers admission, access and treatment in District programs and activities—including but not limited to academic admissions, financial aid, educational services and athletics—and application for District employment!

international.santarosa.edu

D'Youville
www.dyc.edu 800.777.3921
U.S. University Option just minutes from the Canadian border. D'Youville offers majors with an international reputation in Health Care, Business and Liberal Arts. Find out why so many Canadian students are attending D'Youville!
AFFORDABLE...
Merit-Based Scholarships up to $74,000
D'Youville offers significant academic scholarships to qualifying students including transfer students.
ACCELERATED...
Spend Less Time Earning a Higher Degree
D'Youville offers combined degrees that take less time to complete than it would at other schools.
EARNING POWER...
Graduate with More Potential
D'Youville offers dual and sequential degree programs in high-demand career fields. We are a global leader in education & health care programs with a strong, respected reputation.
Canadian Students receive a 20% tuition waiver!
For more information or to schedule a visit
PLEASE CONTACT US NOW
D'YOUVILLE COLLEGE
D'Youville COLLEGE
Educating for life
320 Porter Avenue • Buffalo NY 14201

PRODUCE
EDIT
COMPOSE
VISUAL EFFECTS
AUDIO
CINEMATOGRAPHY
RECORD
DIRECT
NETWORK
DESIGN
COMMUNITY
PORTFOLIO
LIGHTING
GAMES
THEORY
LISTEN
CREATIVE PROCESS
STRATEGY
GOALS
PLANNING
ANIMATION
PROMOTE
PITCH IDEA
CAREER PATH
YOUR FUTURE IN ENTERTAINMENT STARTS HERE.
Visit lafilm.edu or call 323.860.0789 to find out more!
THE LOS ANGELES FILM SCHOOL®
© 2017 The Los Angeles Film School. All rights reserved. The term "The Los Angeles Film School" and The Los Angeles Film School logo are either service marks or registered service marks of The Los Angeles Film School. For more information on our programs and their outcomes, go to lafilm.edu/disclosures. Accredited College, ACCSC. VA-Approved by CSAAVE. Member of the Servicemembers Opportunity College Consortium.
MIX
DEVELOP
TALENT
RENDER
CONCEPTUALIZE
MANAGEMENT
MUSIC
PR
CREATE
IMAGINE
VOLUME
CONNECTIONS
LEARN
THOUGHT
MASTER
CONTRACTS
PLAY
DEGREE

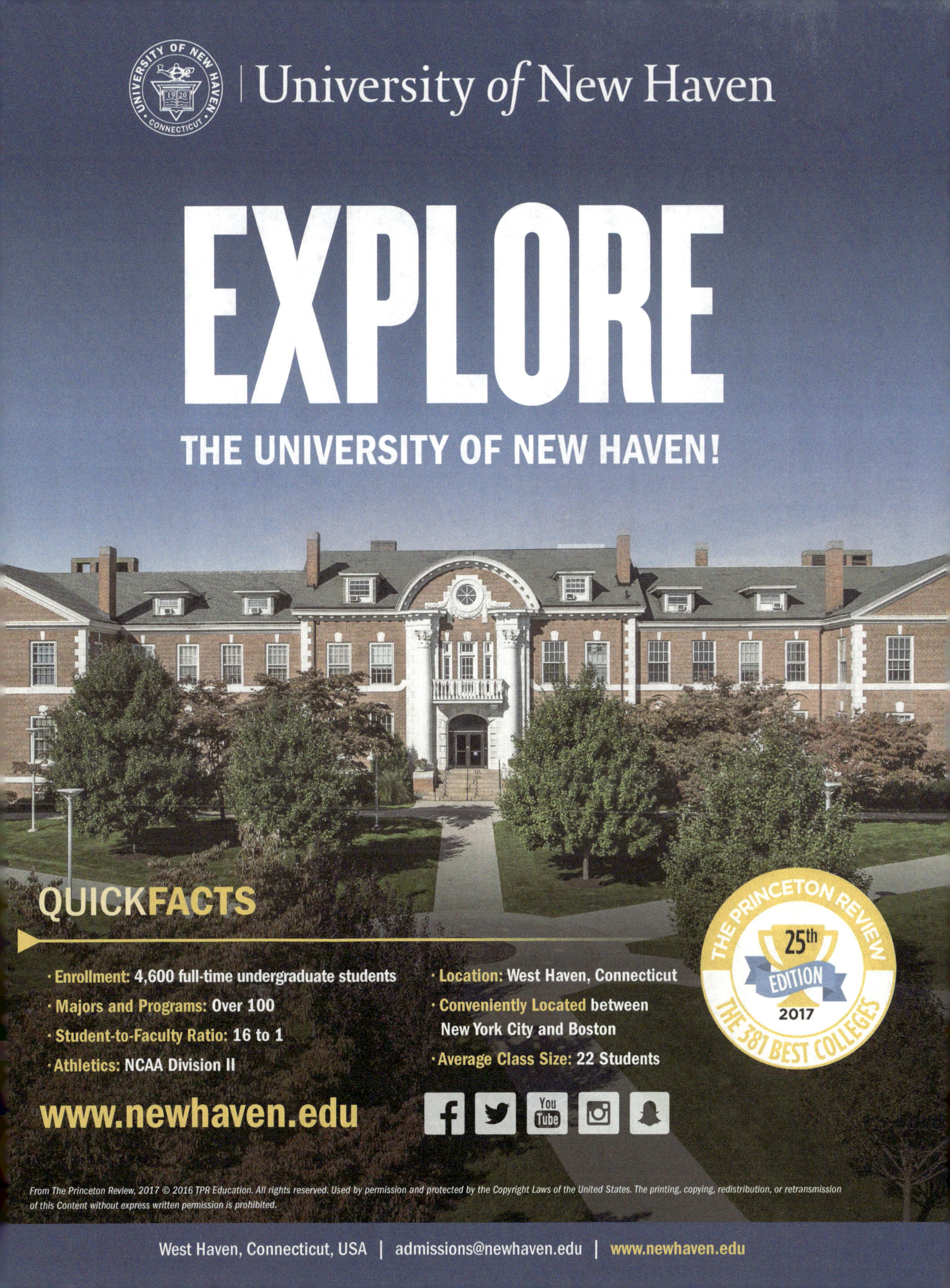
University of New Haven
UNIVERSITY OF NEW HAVEN CONNECTICUT 1920
EXPLORE
THE UNIVERSITY OF NEW HAVEN!
QUICKFACTS
· Enrollment: 4,600 full-time undergraduate students
· Majors and Programs: Over 100
· Student-to-Faculty Ratio: 16 to 1
· Athletics: NCAA Division II
· Location: West Haven, Connecticut
· Conveniently Located between New York City and Boston
· Average Class Size: 22 Students
THE PRINCETON REVIEW 25th EDITION 2017 THE 381 BEST COLLEGES
www.newhaven.edu
From The Princeton Review, 2017 © 2016 TPR Education. All rights reserved. Used by permission and protected by the Copyright Laws of the United States. The printing, copying, redistribution, or retransmission of this Content without express written permission is prohibited.
West Haven, Connecticut, USA | admissions@newhaven.edu | www.newhaven.edu

on the RISE
At our campus without boundaries in downtown Atlanta, we're creating new approaches to higher education and guiding our students to uncommon success.
Widely recognized as one of the nation's most innovative universities, Georgia State is a powerful force for transformation, inspiring our students, our city and our community.
WE'RE CLIMBING HIGHER.
Learn more at GSU.EDU.
Georgia State University
2X RESEARCH GROWTH than the national average
4TH MOST INNOVATIVE UNIVERSITY in the U.S.*
14TH commitment to UNDERGRADUATE TEACHING*
* U.S. News & World Report © 2017 Georgia State University. All rights reserved.

RELATIVITY
SCHOOL
The first [and only] school of its kind
created with a hollywood studio
Our innovative baccalaureate programs are training Hollywood's
next-generation of storytellers and content entrepreneurs.
Film + Digital Content
Entrepreneurship
Art [Production Design]
Acting [Film + Television]
Commercial Dance
Contemporary Musical Theatre + Film
RelativitySchool.org • 800.762.1993
Relativity School is an accredited branch campus of Hussian College.

HOW TO MAKE YOUR PAYMENT

Paying tuition with Paymytuition is safe, fast, and convenient. Follow the simple steps below to complete your payment:

1 **ENTER YOUR INSTITUTION NAME**

Go to **paymytuition.com**. From the drop-down menu, select "Tuition Payment" then enter your payment amount and the country you are paying from.

2 **SELECT PAYMENT METHOD**

Review the payment options provided and select your preferred payment method. Payment options include bank transfers, debit/credit cards in your home currency, electronic and eWallet payments and other local options.

3 **ENTER YOUR DETAILS**

Create your account and enter some basic information including your student number. We will include this information to your payment for easy identification of your payment by your institution.

4 **MAKE YOUR PAYMENT**

Follow the instructions provided to send your funds to **Paymytuition by MTFX** via your selected payment method.

5 **TRACK & CONFIRM**

Track your payment by logging into your **Paymytuition Dashboard** at any time. Receive SMS texts, email status updates, and confirmations of when your payment has been delivered.